EFFECT GRANTS MANAGEMENT

Deborah L. Ward, MA, CFRE
President
Ward and Associates
Winona, Minnesota

JONES AND BARTLETT PUBLISHERS
Sudbury, Massachusetts
BOSTON   TORONTO   LONDON   SINGAPORE

World Headquarters
Jones and Bartlett Publishers
40 Tall Pine Drive
Sudbury, MA 01776
978-443-5000
info@jbpub.com
www.jbpub.com

Jones and Bartlett Publishers
Canada
6339 Ormindale Way
Mississauga, Ontario L5V 1J2
Canada

Jones and Bartlett Publishers
International
Barb House, Barb Mews
London W6 7PA
United Kingdom

Jones and Bartlett's books and products are available through most bookstores and online booksellers. To contact Jones and Bartlett Publishers directly, call 800-832-0034, fax 978-443-8000, or visit our website, www.jbpub.com.

Substantial discounts on bulk quantities of Jones and Bartlett's publications are available to corporations, professional associations, and other qualified organizations. For details and specific discount information, contact the special sales department at Jones and Bartlett via the above contact information or send an email to specialsales@jbpub.com.

This publication is designed to provide accurate and authoritative information in regard to the Subject Matter covered. It is sold with the understanding that the publisher is not engaged in rendering legal, accounting, or other professional service. If legal advice or other expert assistance is required, the service of a competent professional person should be sought.

Production Credits
Publisher: Michael Brown
Associate Editor: Megan Turner
Editorial Assistant: Catie Heverling
Production Director: Amy Rose
Senior Production Editor: Renée Sekerak
Senior Marketing Manager: Sophie Fleck
Manufacturing and Inventory Control Supervisor: Amy Bacus
Composition: Auburn Associates, Inc.
Cover Design: Kristin E. Parker
Cover Image: © Yuri Arcurs/ShutterStock, Inc.
Printing and Binding: Malloy Incorporated
Cover Printing: Malloy Incorporated

Library of Congress Cataloging-in-Publication Data
Ward, Deborah, 1957-
    Effective grants management / by Deborah L. Ward.
        p. cm.
    Includes bibliographical references and index.
    ISBN-13: 978-0-7637-4984-2
    ISBN-10: 0-7637-4984-2
    1. Fund raising. 2. Proposal writing for grants. 3. Grants-in-aid. I. Title.
    HG177.W367 2010
    658.15'224—dc22

                                                        2009033479

6048

Printed in the United States of America
13 12 11 10 09   10 9 8 7 6 5 4 3 2 1

Contents

I have known Deborah Ward (Deb) for many years; it seems like forever although we're both still youngsters. The first time that I met Deb, I was immediately impressed by her open and easy to follow style of communication. At the time, we both belonged to the American Association of Grant Professionals and used this annual craft development and collegial meeting venue to grow our friendship. Deb possesses a high level of grant-related knowledge, expertise, and skills. Also the author of *Writing Grant Proposals That Win, Third Edition* (Jones and Bartlett Publishers) where she gives step-by-step instructions and clear examples of how to write winning grant proposals, it is with this same experience-driven approach that Deb authored this book, *Effective Grants Management*. Using her decades of grants management experience, she begins this book with basic and easy to understand opening chapters. For the reader just tasked with managing incoming grant awards, Deb writes first about the foundation of the grants management process. The lineup of chapters continues with incorporating grants management into your proposal; negotiating the grant award; coordinating tasks; evaluation; audits; Federal and private funder expectations; closeout procedures, and most importantly, problem solving. *Effective Grants Management* is a desktop "must have" for every grant writer and grants manager. When a grant award is mismanaged, everyone is assumed guilty until an audit proves otherwise. Don't be the grant professional appearing in headline news because you didn't know or didn't ask about the management process and follow its implementation diligently. Get informed! Wise up! Buy and read this book!

Dr. Beverly A. Browning (Dr. Bev aka the Grant Doctor or Grant Guru)
Author of 26 grant-related publications including *Grant Writing for Dummies* (2001, 2005, and 2008), John Wiley & Sons, Inc.

Acknowledgments

First, I want to thank everyone at Jones and Bartlett, especially Jeremy Spiegel, for giving me the chance to write another book and for your patience while I worked on this manuscript. I am honored to be a published author and have to admit, seeing a book with my name on the cover is very exciting!

Second, I want to thank Ginny Lays, Jeannie Floyd, and Bev Browning for your friendship and for sharing your amazing skills as grants professionals. I loved Ginny's reaction when I told her I was writing a new book about grants management. She said "Yuck" (referring to the topic, not the content of my book, I'm sure) but then quickly added it was a needed subject and heartily congratulated me. Jeannie has been kind enough to let me visit her great home in Florida and to also ask her all kinds of questions related to grants. Bev is an amazing colleague with a copious amount of knowledge in this field and a sunny smile. I consider them all grants experts, and I am so impressed with their professional skills and especially glad to call them my friends.

Third, to my colleagues in my professional network who made it so easy for me to send an e-mail or make a phone call and get the documents or information that I was looking for to include in this book. Thank you Matt Rearick for taking the time to answer my questions about evaluation.

And last, but not least, thank you to my family. My parents and my brother who were so proud when my first book was published and took pictures at a book signing. Hopefully we can do it again with this one! And, with love for Megan. I know that wherever you end up on this planet, you will make a difference.

Deborah L. Ward, MA, CFRE, is a nationally recognized proposal writing consultant for education and nonprofit clients and has her own business, Ward and Associates, based in Winona, MN. She provides grant development services that include: project development, prospect research (federal, state, corporate and foundation funding sources); RFP analysis; writing and editing of proposals; proposal submission; and evaluation of grants programs. Her clients have included school districts, education service agencies, foundations, higher education institutions, education, vendors, local governments and nonprofit organizations including a museum, an EMS organization, a hospital, arts organizations, and a leadership program.

Ms. Ward provides grant seeking and proposal writing workshops across the United States and has presented at local, state, national, and international conferences. She has presented two workshops for government employees in Guam and taught a "Grantwriting for Teachers" course at Trinity College in Washington D.C.

Ms. Ward is a contributing monthly columnist for *eSchool News* and a former columnist for *Education Grants Alert*. Her articles have appeared in *Pro Principal, Board and Administrator, School Planning and Management, Technology and Learning, T.H.E. Funding Source*, and *Principal*. She has been interviewed for several publications including *Education Week* and *Advancing Philanthropy*. In 2005, her book, *Writing Grant Proposals that Win, 3rd Edition* was published by Jones and Bartlett Publishers. She is currently working on her second book about grants management with an expected publication date this fall.

She has over 20 years of experience in the development field in the areas of grantsmanship, individual donor and corporate solicitations, direct mail appeals, special events, and annual funds. In 1999, she received her Master of Arts degree in philanthropy and development from Saint Mary's University of Minnesota. She has the Certified Fund Raising Executive designation from the Association of Fund Raising Professionals and participated in their Executive Leadership Institute.

Chapter 1

Introduction to Grants Management

There are six types of grants that require management. They are:

1. Capital grants that are generally for endowment, building, equipment, or construction.
2. General operating grants that are for the everyday operations of an organization.
3. Program/project grants that are for a specific activity or plan within an organization that are usually time limited.
4. Start-up grants that cover the costs of starting a new project or organization.
5. Technical assistance grants that support an organization's development or infrastructure needs.
6. Planning grants that support the planning stages of a future project.

What is grants management? It is a combination of a definition of a time frame and the activities that take place during that time frame. Grants management is the phase of the grantsmanship process that begins when an applicant signs an agreement with a grantor (funder) to accept a grant award and becomes a grantee.

Grant award offers can be made by letter or through a form or in an informal way. In some cases, grantors will notify applicants of a grant award via a telephone call or email message. This informal type of notification can be used by private funders such as foundations.

When a grant award is accepted, the implementation of the project begins on a specific date, and then the grantee has to manage the grant from both a programmatic and a financial standpoint until the final date of the grant award period.

The grants management process ends for a specific grant when it is closed out. This is typically when all grant funds have been spent and accounted for, and the end date of the grant award period has been reached. Projects can, however, continue beyond this end date, and often do with funding from additional grantors and/or organizations building the expenses into their annual budgets.

Typically, many grant awards will cover a 12-month period except in the case of continuation funding or multiyear grants. This means that the grants management process will also cover a 12-month period. Some grantors will allow grantees a 3-month period after the end date to submit their final programmatic and financial reports. Grantees who do not submit their final reports can lose the final payment of their grant award and may in fact jeopardize their chances of future funding from a grantor.

What types of activities does managing a grant include? Each grantor requires different activities during the grants management phase of a project; however, in general, the following are expected to be carried out by the grantee:

- Following all of the terms and conditions associated with the grant
- Fulfilling reporting requirements throughout the grant award period
- Making requests for changes to an award in a timely manner before the project end, if necessary
- Fulfilling financial reporting requirements
- Accounting for grant revenue and expenditures
- Submitting final reports in a timely manner
- Following closeout procedures as stipulated by the grantor
- Conducting the grants management process in an ethical manner

Effective Grants Management

It is critical that a grantee exercise effective grants management strategies for a variety of reasons. Most important is that a grantee can lose funding during the implementation process of a project if he or she is not effectively managing the grant.

Grantees need to fully understand the relationship that they are entering into when they sign the award agreement. In addition to this relationship with the grantor, grantees who accept grant awards are entering into a legal contract with them. In exchange for financial support (the grant award), grantees are promising that they will honor the intent of the project and implement it to the best of their ability as outlined in the proposal that was submitted. They will work towards achieving the objectives and goals as outlined, and they will conduct an evaluation to determine whether they successfully did so. In addition, they will spend the award funds as delineated in the line items listed in the budget. If a grantee chooses not to work toward the objectives, evaluating their success and spending the money appropriately, it can be considered a breach of contract, and grantors can request that funds be returned or they can stop the funding at any point during the project implementation.

As already mentioned in regard to final report submission, the mismanagement of grants can have both immediate and long-term negative consequences for a grantee that include loss of funding from both current and would-be future grantors, damage to one's reputation, and in the most severe cases, criminal prosecution.

Definition of Terms in This Book

Applicant refers to a group or organization that submits a proposal or application and requests grant funding for a project.

Grantee refers to a group or organization that accepts a grant award from a funder.

Grantor and *funder* are used interchangeably in this book and refer to a federal or state agency or a foundation (private, family, and/or corporate) that reviews grant applications and selects projects to be funded.

Monies or *funds* are the dollars received by a grantee to implement the project.

Matching funds are financial contributions to a project made by the grantee and/or collaborative partners.

In-kind contributions are matching funds and are usually items or services that have a dollar value.

This book will cover the following areas related to grants management:

- How to build grants management into an initial grant proposal
- Negotiating a grant award and acceptance procedures
- Coordinating grants management tasks
- Audits and monitoring visits
- Evaluation
- Closeout procedures
- Grants management of federal grants
- Grants management of private funder grants
- Ethical issues related to grants management
- Problem solving

Chapter 2

Building Grants Management Into the Proposal

Although grants management is the phase of the grantsmanship process that comes after the proposal is submitted and funded, it is possible and advisable to build grants management into the proposal itself. Successful grants management is a critical piece of the entire project puzzle, and in order for all of the pieces to fit, the following components are necessary in a proposal:

- Solid methodology
- Clear objectives
- Competent personnel
- Comprehensive evaluation plan
- Budget that covers all costs of the project

Solid Methodology

A proposal should contain a solid plan of operation. *All* stakeholders in the project—not just staff—should discuss staffing needs to successfully carry out a project as well as specific activities that will need to occur in order to meet the stated goals and objectives.

The methodology section of a proposal should explain *how* a project will be carried out. For example, a project to increase the number of food donations being made to a food bank throughout the year rather than just during the holidays could include strategies to raise the public's awareness of the incidence of hunger in the community (e.g., using newspaper articles, radio spots, billboards, and television coverage), ways to encourage more people to donate food (e.g., using letter campaigns, possible incentives for donating), and ways to make donating food more convenient for people (e.g., drop-off locations for food donations throughout the community, adding a monetary donation to household grocery bills, making door-to-door food collections). The example food donation project could also culminate in community notification about the results of their donations by print and media coverage of the amount of food that was collected and distributed as well as human interest stories about individuals and families who received food donations.

Clear Objectives

Objectives should be clear and measurable, and if reached, allow a project goal to be met. They should reflect the results of a project, but not the activities (these are covered in the methodology section described previously). Depending on the type of project being carried out, there are at least four types of objectives to select. Some projects will include a mix of the four, while others may only have one type of objective.

The first type of objective is a *performance* objective. This objective sets a specific level of performance for a specific type of behavior. Here is an example of a performance objective:

> *At the completion of the project, paramedics will score 15 points higher on the posttest compared to their results on the pretest.*

The second type of objective is a *behavioral* objective. This objective focuses on the project participants and describes cognitive performance. Here is an example of this type of objective:

> *At the end of the treatment program, adolescents will reduce the number of inappropriate emotional outbursts by 50%.*

The third type of an objective is a *product* objective. This objective is used when a specific product will be designed or created as a result of the project. Types of products can include policies, procedures, publications (articles, reports, etc.), training manuals, and curriculum. Here is a sample objective:

> *By the end of the first year of the project, 8th-grade history teachers will develop a 6-week curriculum that examines the roles of women during the Civil War.*

The final type of objective is a *process* objective. This objective will describe a process or procedure that is going to occur that measures the progress of the project. Here is an example:

By the end of the first year, fifteen 1-week internships will be established with local employers for the middle school students, representing half of the project goal of thirty.

Competent Personnel

In addition to implementing the project, personnel will often be responsible for collecting data for evaluation and reporting purposes and for completing programmatic and fiscal reports required by the funder. Therefore, it is important that these staff members not only have skills to function as project managers, but also have the ability to complete required paperwork that is a part of the grants management process.

Comprehensive Evaluation Plan

As most seasoned proposal writers know, there is a direct relationship between a project's clearly stated and measurable objectives and the evaluation plan for the project. As stated above in the Clear Objectives section of this chapter, objectives lead to project goals being met and reflect the results of the project. The evaluation measures the success of reaching stated objectives and, ultimately, enables a grantee to reach a conclusion about whether or not the goal was met. Including a comprehensive evaluation plan in the proposal makes the job of managing the grant easy from the beginning of the project. Solid evaluation plans will inform staff about the kinds of data that need to be collected during the implementation process and the frequency of data collection. These plans also show funders what types of tools and analyses will be performed in order to gauge the success of their investment in a proposed project and show staff what will be expected during the project.

Adequate Budget

The budget is the numerical representation of the information described in the methodology, personnel, and evaluation sections of a grant proposal. Funders assume that all of the costs associated with these sections are going to appear in the project budget. Grantees can submit a revised budget at the request of a funder. However, grantees cannot submit a revised budget if they forgot to include expenses in the budget that were submitted with the original proposal.

Grant managers should carefully review all expenses in the budget and be sure not to overlook any that might make managing the grant difficult. Here are some examples of costs that might be overlooked and could impact the grants management process:

1. *Time*—If salary is an allowable budget item, be sure to factor in time so staff can complete the programmatic and fiscal reports required by the funder.
2. *Evaluation report costs*—Any costs associated with the production and/or dissemination of evaluation reports.
3. *Other costs*—If they are an allowable budget item, expenses associated with an external evaluator in addition to salary, such as travel, must be included. Also, costs associated with the creation or utilization of evaluation tools should be in the budget. Two examples of potentially overlooked costs include those for any long-distance phone interviews and child care if it is provided for face-to-face interviews with project participants.

Chapter Summary

Planning a project in detail and writing a comprehensive proposal are two ways to make the grants management process easier when a grant award is made. Thinking carefully about the project methodology, personnel, and evaluation in advance will help to avoid problems during implementation. All costs should be included in the budget so there are no unexpected expenditures when the project is occurring.

Chapter 3

Negotiation and Acceptance Procedures

The weeks, and in some cases, months, after a proposal is submitted can seem to last forever. In some requests for proposals and funding guidelines, funders will clearly state the time frame for funding decisions to be made. But there can be a variety of issues that can arise to delay the notification process. It is best for applicants to wait for at least the amount of time designated before contacting a funder to find out if a decision has been made.

The Selection Process

Federal funders may use a one-, two-, or even three-tiered process in order to select projects for funding. These processes typically use groups of reviewers who have expertise in the field of the grant program. The reviewers score proposals and do so on either an individual or group basis. Proposals are eliminated when the scores are too low, and those with the highest scores are recommended for funding. Agency or department staff review the recommendations and release the final list of funded projects.

Private funders, however, use a different process. Often, program officers review the proposals that are submitted and select those that they feel will be of most interest to the members of the foundation board. Private funders also use selection committees to do the review of proposals. Typically, the review and selection process takes less time than it does for public funders. Many private funders have several deadlines throughout the year and can make funding decisions within 8 weeks.

Negotiating the Grant Award

What happens if a funder offers less money than the amount included in the proposal? What if the funder requests that the activities or the budget in the proposal be revised in order to receive funding? The most important key to these situations is to take time to respond to the funder. Do not make a hasty decision based on the money alone.

Applicants who are asked to make changes should request time to make a decision and must be prepared to negotiate if changes need to be made to the project and/or the budget. Grants managers should examine the original proposal carefully and consider how a reduction in funds would impact the project.

Will objectives need to be revised? If there is less money and this means that some activities will be dropped, will the same objectives still be possible? If activities are dropped, this will more than likely have an impact on the methodology.

Sometimes funders will consider adjustments to activities and objectives if a lesser amount of money is received. Unfortunately, other funders will expect that all of the activities and objectives in the original proposal will still be carried out with reduced funds. When applicants are offered thousands of dollars less than the amount they requested or only receive an offer of half of the amount they requested, they need to seriously consider if they want to accept the grant award. They must keep in mind that their organization will need to absorb any additional expenses that might come up if the budget submitted with the proposal was a true representation of the project costs.

If a funder is not willing to negotiate any activities or budget expenses, the applicant might have to make the unpleasant decision to decline the grant award. However, it is wiser to do this than accept a lesser amount of money and still try to implement the project as it was stated in the original proposal.

Notification of Funding

Funders use a variety of methods to notify applicants that their project has been selected for funding. The National Institutes of Health and the U.S. Department of Education, for example, use a Notice of Award form. In contrast, private funders will use letters, email communication, or even a telephone call to notify an organization of their funding award. As examples, see the Winona County Community Foundation grant agreement (**Figure 3–1**) and the award package of the Lancaster Emergency Medical Services Association (**Figure 3–2**). It received a U.S. Department of Homeland Security Assistance to Firefighters grant in 2006.

May 1, 2007

I _____ accept the Winona Community Foundation grant award for the amount of **AMOUNT**.

I agree that these dollars may only be used by **ORGANIZATION** for **PURPOSE**. If for some reason the program may cease to exist before grant dollars are spent I will contact the Winona Community Foundation to discuss our alternatives.

I agree that the Winona Community Foundation will be mentioned as a funder and partner in publicity about this project.

I agree that a report of the program progress must be received at the Winona Community Foundation when the project is completed or by **May 1, 2008**–whichever is sooner. The report should address how program objectives were met along with any challenges or successes that occurred along the way.

Reports are also encouraged to include digital photos that could be used in Winona Community Foundation's annual report or for further publicity by the Foundation.

I agree to contact the Winona Community Foundation if there is any leadership change in the program, major project or budget changes, or any other changes in contact information.

_____
(name & title printed)

_____
(signature)   (date)

_____
(Contact info – phone, e-mail, address)

_____

Figure 3–1 *Winona Community Foundation agreement.*
Source: Reprinted with permission from Winona Community Foundation.

Panel Review

Office of Grants and Training
Preparedness Directorate
U.S. Department of Homeland Security
Washington, D.C. 20531

Mr. C. Robert May
Lancaster Emergency Medical Services Association
1829 Lincoln Highway East
Lancaster, Pennsylvania 17602-3323

Re: Grant No. EMW-2006-FG-10076

Dear Mr. May:

On behalf of the Office of Grants and Training, I am pleased to inform you that your grant application submitted under the FY 2006 Assistance to Firefighters Grant has been approved. Along with the U.S. Fire Administration and the Federal Emergency Management Agency, we carry out the federal responsibilities of administering your grant. The approved project costs total to $47,300.00. The Federal share is $37,840.00 of the approved amount and your share of the costs is $9,460.00.

As part of your award package, you will find Grant Agreement Articles. Please make sure you read and understand the Articles as they outline the terms and conditions of your Grant award. Maintain a copy of these documents for your official file. **You establish acceptance of the Grant and Grant Agreement Articles when you request and receive any of the Federal Grant funds awarded to you.**

The first step in requesting your grant funds is to confirm your correct Direct Deposit Information. Please go on-line to the AFG eGrants system at **www.firegrantsupport.com** and if you have not done so, complete and submit your SF 1199A, Direct Deposit Sign-up Form. Please forward the original, completed SF 1199A, Direct Deposit Sign-up Form, signed by your organization and the banking institution to the address below:

> Department of Homeland Security
> Emergency Preparedness and Response Directorate (FEMA)
> Grants Management Branch
> 500 C Street, SW, Room 334
> Washington, DC 20472
>
> Attn: Assistance to Firefighters Grant Program

After your SF 1199A is reviewed and you receive an email indicating the form is approved, you will be able to request payments online. Remember, you should basically request funds when you have an immediate cash need (i.e. you have a bill in-hand that is due within 30 days).

If you are using AFG funds to replace used or outdated equipment, you should be aware of an opportunity to dispose of your old equipment in a manner that will benefit other fire departments. The Office of Grants and Training has recently expanded its Homeland Defense Equipment Reuse Program (HDER) by partnering with the non-profit organization Helping Our Own, Inc. Helping Our Own refurbishes or recycles used firefighting equipment and makes it available to fire departments at no cost. To make an equipment contribution to the HDER program, contact Mr. Jerry Kaufman at 1-877-446-6435 to arrange to have your used equipment picked up. For further information about the HDER program go to www.rkb.mipt.org and find the HDER program link under "Additional Information," or go to the 2006 frequently asked questions (FAQs) for the AFG located at www.firegrantsupport.com.

If you have any questions or concerns regarding the awards process, donations, or how to request your grant funds, please call 1-866-274-0960.

Sincerely,

Tracy A. Henke
Assistant Secretary
Office of Grants and Training

Figure 3–2 *Lancaster Emergency Medical Services Association Department of Homeland Security Award package.*

Source: Reprinted with permission of Lancaster Emergency Medical Services Association.

Panel Review

Agreement Articles

U.S. Department of Homeland Security
Washington, D.C. 20531

AGREEMENT ARTICLES

ASSISTANCE TO FIREFIGHTERS GRANT PROGRAM - Operations and Safety program

GRANTEE: Lancaster Emergency Medical Services Association

PROGRAM: Operations and Safety

AGREEMENT NUMBER: EMW-2006-FG-10076

AMENDMENT NUMBER:

TABLE OF CONTENTS

Article I - Project Description

The purpose of the Assistance to Firefighters Program is to protect the health and safety of the public and firefighting personnel against fire and fire-related hazards. After careful consideration, DHS has determined that the grantee's project submitted as part of the grantee's application, and detailed in the project narrative as well as the request details section of the application – including budget information – was consistent with the program's purpose and worthy of award. The grantee shall perform the work described in the approved grant application as itemized in the request details section of the application and further described in the grant application's narrative. These sections of the application are made a part of these grant agreement articles by reference. The grantee may not change or make any material deviations from the approved scope of work outlined in the above referenced sections of the application without prior written approval.

Figure 3–2 *continues*

Panel Review

However, in keeping with this year's program guidance, grantees that have grant funds left over after completing the approved scope of work prior to the end of the period of performance have three options for the use of the excess funds: 1) they may return the unused funds to the Federal government, 2) they may use a maximum of $5,000 to expand the activities for which they were awarded, or 3) create or expand an existing fire prevention program. Grantees are encouraged to review the program guidance for more information in this area.

Article II - Grantee Concurrence

By requesting and receiving Federal grant funds provided by this grant program, the grantee accepts and agrees to abide by the terms and conditions of the grant as set forth in this document and the documents identified below. All documents submitted as part of the application are made a part of this agreement by reference.

Article III - Period of Performance

The period of performance shall be from **03-NOV-06 to 02-NOV-07**.

The grant funds are available to the grantee for obligation only during the period of performance of the grant award. The grantee is not authorized to incur new obligations after the expiration date unless the grantee has requested, and DHS has approved, a new expiration date. The grantee has 90 days after period of performance to incur costs associated with closeout or to pay for obligations incurred during period of performance. Award expenditures are for the purposes detailed in the approved grant application only. The grantee cannot transfer funds or assets purchased with grant funds to other agencies or departments without prior written approval from DHS.

Article IV - Amount Awarded

The amount of the award is detailed on the Obligating Document for Award attached to these articles. Following are the budgeted estimates for each object classes of this grant (including Federal share plus grantee match):

Personnel	$0.00
Fringe Benefits	$0.00
Travel	$0.00
Equipment	$47,300.00
Supplies	$0.00
Contractual	$0.00
Construction	$0.00
Other	$0.00
Indirect Charges	$0.00
Total	$47,300.00

Article V - Requests for Advances or Reimbursements

Grant payments under the Assistance to Firefighters Grant Program are made on an advance or reimbursable basis for immediate cash needs. When the grantee needs grant funds and has obtained a user account, the grantee fills out the on-line Request for Advance or Reimbursement. If the grantee has not obtained a user account, an account may be obtained by calling the help desk at 1-866-274-0960.

Article VI - Budget Changes

Generally, grantees may make changes in funding levels between the object classes (as detailed in Article IV above), as long as the grant's project or scope of work is accomplished. The grant's scope of work is outlined in the project narrative and in the request details of the grant application. The only exception to this provision is for grants where the Federal share is in excess of $100,000. In grants where the Federal share exceeds $100,000,

Figure 3–2 *continued*

the funding levels of the object classes can be changed, but if the cumulative changes exceed ten (10) percent of the total budget, changes must be pre-approved. The provisions of this article are not applicable to changes in the budgeted line-items listed in the request details section of the application.

Article VII - Financial Reporting

The Request for Advance or Reimbursement mentioned above will also be used for interim financial reporting purposes. At the end of the performance period, or upon completion of the grantee's program narrative, the grantee must complete, on-line, a final financial report that is required to close out the grant. The Financial Status Report is due within 90 days after the end of the performance period.

Article VIII - Performance Reports

The grantee must submit a semi-annual and a final performance report to DHS. The final performance report should provide a short narrative on what the grantee accomplished with the grant funds and any benefits derived there from. The semi-annual report is due six months after the award date.

Article IX - DHS Officials

Program Officer: Tom Harrington, Deputy Chief of the Grants Program Office, is the Program Officer for this grant program. The Program Officer is responsible for the technical monitoring of the stages of work and technical performance of the activities described in the approved grant application.

Grants Assistance Officer: Christine Torres is the Assistance Officer for this grant program. The Assistance Officer is the Federal official responsible for negotiating, administering, and executing all grant business matters.

Grants Management Branch POC: Marie Rogers is the point of contact for this grant award and shall be contacted for all financial and administrative grant business matters. If you have any questions regarding your grant please call 703-605-0631.

Article X - Other Terms and Conditions

Pre-award costs directly applicable to the awarded grant are allowable if approved in writing by the DHS Program Office.

Article XI - General Provisions

The following are hereby incorporated into this agreement by reference:

44 CFR, Emergency Management and Assistance

Part 7	Nondiscrimination in Federally-Assisted Programs
Part 13	Uniform administrative requirements for grants and cooperative agreements to state and local governments
Part 17	Government-wide Debarment and Suspension (Non-procurement) and Government-wide Requirements for Drug-free Workplace (Grants)
Part 18	New Restrictions on Lobbying

31 CFR 205.6 Funding Techniques

OMB Circular A-21 Cost Principles for Educational Institutions

OMB Circular A-87 Cost Principles for State/local Governments, Indian tribes

Figure 3–2 *continues*

Panel Review

OMB Circular A-122 Cost Principles for Non-Profit Organizations

OMB Circular A-102	Uniform Administrative Requirements for Grants and Agreements With State and Local Governments Assistance to Firefighters Grant Application and Assurances contained therein.
OMB Circular A-110	Uniform Administrative Requirements for Grants and Agreements With Institutions of Higher Education, Hospitals, and Other NonProfit Organizations Assistance to Firefighters Grant Application and Assurances contained therein.

Article XII- Audit Requirements

All grantees must follow the audit requirements of OMB Circular A-133, Audits of States, Local Governments, and Non-Profit Organizations. The main requirement of this OMB Circular is that grantees that expend $500,000.00 or more in Federal funds (from all Federal sources) must have a single audit performed in accordance with the circular.

As a condition of receiving funding under this grant program, you must agree to maintain grant files and supporting documentation for three years upon the official closeout of your grant. You must also agree to make your grant files, books, and records available for an audit by DHS, the General Accounting Office (GAO), or their duly authorized representatives to assess the accomplishments of the grant program or to ensure compliance with any requirement of the grant program.

Article XIII- Additional Requirements (if applicable)

- Vehicle awardees for FY 2006 will be required to include a performance bond as part of the contract with the vehicle manufacturer. The performance bond MUST include a delivery date to be acceptable under this requirement. Extensions to a grant's period of performance may not be considered if a performance bond is not included in the purchase contract. Note: This is a new requirement for this program year.
- Grantees that are the hosts of regional projects as provided for in the annual program guidance will not be responsible for equipment purchased with grant funds if that equipment is disbursed to other first-responder organizations under a memorandum of understanding which places the responsibility for the equipment in the hands of the recipient.

Additional Requirements if applicable

This grant award was reduced by $131,566. The approved amount is for 48 Helmets @ $93.00 not 125. The approved amount is for 48 Gloves @ $40.00 not 125. The approved amount is for 48 pants @ $240.00 not 125 @$389.00 and 48 coats @ $360.00 not 125 @ $812.00 as indicated in the initial application. The reduction has already been made in the grant award and in the application as approved by the grantee (Suzanne Reiley) via email on October 25, 2006. The total project cost was reduced per the program office comments from $178,866 to $47,300. The federal share was reduced from $143,0963 to $44,935. The applicant's match was reduced from $35,773 to $2,365.

Figure 3–2 *continued*

Panel Review

FEDERAL EMERGENCY MANAGEMENT AGENCY
OBLIGATING DOCUMENT FOR AWARD/AMENDMENT

1a. AGREEMENT NO. EMW-2006-FG-10076	2. AMENDMENT NO. 0	3. RECIPIENT NO. 23-2840702		4. TYPE OF ACTION AWARD	5. CONTROL NO. W437660N

6. RECIPIENT NAME AND ADDRESS Lancaster Emergency Medical Services Association 1829 Lincoln Highway East Lancaster Pennsylvania, 17602-3323	7. ISSUING OFFICE AND ADDRESS ODP/Financial and Grants Management Division 500 C Street, S.W., Room 350 Washington DC, 20472 POC: Marie Rogers 703-605-0631	8. PAYMENT OFFICE AND ADDRESS ODP/Financial Services Branch 500 C Street, S.W., Room 723 Washington DC, 20472

9. NAME OF RECIPIENT PROJECT OFFICER C. Robert May	PHONE NO. 7174814841X14	10. NAME OF PROJECT COORDINATOR Tom Harrington	PHONE NO. 1-866-274-0960

11. EFFECTIVE DATE OF THIS ACTION 03-NOV-06	12. METHOD OF PAYMENT SF-270	13. ASSISTANCE ARRANGEMENT Cost Sharing	14. PERFORMANCE PERIOD From:03-NOV-06 To:02-NOV-07

Budget Period
From:20-OCT-06 To:30-SEP-07

15. DESCRIPTION OF ACTION
a. (Indicate funding data for awards or financial changes)

PROGRAM NAME ACRONYM	CFDA NO.	ACCOUNTING DATA (AACS CODE) XXXX-XXX-XXXXXX-XXXXX-XXXX-XXXX-X	PRIOR TOTAL AWARD	AMOUNT AWARDED THIS ACTION + OR (-)	CURRENT TOTAL AWARD	CUMMULATIVE NON-FEDERAL COMMITMENT
AFG	97.044	2007-62-0632RE-63000000-4101-R	$0.00	$37,840.00	$37,840.00	$9,460.00
		TOTALS	$0.00	$37,840.00	$37,840.00	$9,460.00

b. To describe changes other than funding data or financial changes, attach schedule and check here.
N/A

16a. FOR NON-DISASTER PROGRAMS: RECIPIENT IS REQUIRED TO SIGN AND RETURN THREE (3) COPIES OF THIS DOCUMENT TO FEMA (See Block 7 for address)

Assistance to Firefighters Grant recipients are not required to sign and return copies of this document. However, recipients should print and keep a copy of this document for their records.

16b. FOR DISASTER PROGRAMS: RECIPIENT IS NOT REQUIRED TO SIGN

This assistance is subject to terms and conditions attached to this award notice or by incorporated reference in program legislation cited above.

17. RECIPIENT SIGNATORY OFFICIAL (Name and Title) N/A	DATE N/A
18. FEMA SIGNATORY OFFICIAL (Name and Title) Sheila Parker Darby	DATE 02-NOV-06

Go Back

Figure 3–2 *continued*

Accepting a Grant Award

Typically, terms and conditions of a grant award are sent with the grant agreement (see **Figure 3–3** for the Pennsylvania Department of Public Welfare agreement). Grant awards should never be accepted without a full understanding of the responsibilities attached to them. A potential grantee should read all acceptance documents carefully (especially the terms and conditions) and should contact the funder if there are any questions about the responsibilities of a grantee. In some cases, depending on the complexity of the acceptance documents, it might be a good idea to have an attorney review them. (See **Figure 3–4** for terms and conditions for the U.S. Army Research Office, **Figure 3–5** for the South Dakota Arts Council, **Figure 3–6** for the Corporation of National and Community Service, and **Figure 3–7** for revisions to the terms and conditions of the National Science Foundation.)

Before accepting a grant award, the grant manager should be sure to make a note of the dates of the grant period (the most common period is for 12 months), the start and end dates, and the dates for all programmatic and fiscal reports. He or she should mark the calendar with these dates immediately in order to manage the grant effectively. Also, any expenses that are incurred before the start date are the responsibility of the grantee organization.

In addition to dates, grantees must pay close attention to the information related to the payment of the grant award. Funders handle payments in a variety of ways, including:

- Full payment of the grant award at the beginning of the project
- Quarterly payments of the grant award, which might be split evenly or staggered
- Payment of the grant award based on reimbursement with receipts for expenses being submitted and checks being sent 1–3 months later or transferring funds electronically

The most common form of payments is the reimbursement system. This means that a grantee organization must have the ability to spend funds of its own to cover project expenses and the ability to wait for those funds to be reimbursed. See **Figure 3–8** for a request for advance or reimbursement form used by federal grantors.

The grant manager must check the acceptance paperwork to see if an extension of the project is allowable, as well as for the process for requesting an extension. Some funders will require extensions to be requested a few months before the end date of the project. If there is no information in writing about extensions, the manager should consider calling the funder and asking about it. Typically, funders of small grant awards do not allow extensions to projects. Although one should make every attempt to conduct the project within the designated dates, it is helpful to know that if necessary, an extension to complete the project and spend all of the grant dollars can be requested. However, a request for an extension can be denied by a funder.

GRANT AGREEMENT

Applicants: Do not complete this portion of the grant agreement. Please review the entire document and sign and submit the third page of this document only.

This GRANT AGREEMENT is made this _____ day of _____ 2007, between the COMMONWEALTH OF PENNSYLVANIA, DEPARTMENT OF PUBLIC WELFARE ("Department"), and [enter grantee name] ("Grantee"), operating at [enter grantee address].

WITNESSETH:

WHEREAS, the Department of Public Welfare, created by Act 390, approved July 13, 1957, P.L. 852, is responsible for the administration of public assistance programs in the Commonwealth (62 P.S. §403); and

WHEREAS, Section 205 of the Public Welfare Code, 62 P.S. §205, authorizes the Department to make grants of appropriated funds to programs in fields in which the Department has responsibility; and

WHEREAS, the Department expects to allocate $[enter grant amount] from funds expected to be appropriated for the Children's Trust Fund Program; and

WHEREAS, the Grantee will operate the program described in detail in Rider 2 to this grant, which program meets the Department's standards; and

WHEREAS, the Grantee was selected to receive this grant in accordance with the Department's established grant policy and procedure.

NOW, THEREFORE, the parties hereto, intending to be legally bound, hereby agree as follows:

1. The term of this grant shall be from November 1, 2007 to October 31, 2010.

2. The Grantee shall use the funds granted hereunder to faithfully implement the conditions of this grant and operate the program described in Rider 2, subject to the terms and conditions contained herein.

3. The services described in Paragraph 2 above shall be provided in conformity with:

Rider 1	Payment Provisions
Rider 2	Work Statement
Rider 3	Budget
Rider 4	Local Match Verification Letter
Rider 5	State and Federal Funding Assurance
Rider 6	Standard Contract Terms and Conditions
Rider 7	DPW Addendum to Standard Contract Terms and Conditions
Rider 8	Audit Clause "A–E"
Rider 9	Lobbying Certification and Disclosure
Rider 10	Commonwealth Travel Rates

(continues)

Figure 3–3 *Pennsylvania Department of Public Welfare Grant agreement.*
Source: Pennsylvania Department of Public Welfare.

Grant Agreement   2

4. The Riders listed above, as they may be applicable to this grant, are hereby attached and made a part of this Grant Agreement.

5. Grantees shall cooperate and participate with the Grantor in periodic monitoring and evaluation activities for the purpose of verifying that all grant requirements are met.

6. The Grantee will complete and submit program and expenditure reports as required by the Grantor on forms approved by the Grantor. Any unexpended funds must be returned by the Grantee to the Grantor with the fourth-quarter/year-end report within 60 days of the end of each year.

7. At the beginning of each new grant year, a review of the previous grant year will be conducted by the CTF Board to determine continuation of the grant for the second and third grant years before payments are initiated.

8. The CTF Logo must be displayed on all publications and documents produced by the Grantee for the funded program. Recognition or credit must be given that the Grantee's program is funded all or in part by CTF. News releases pertaining to this project must be forwarded to the CTF program office.

9. Subject to the availability of State and Federal funds, the Department will pay the Grantee, in accordance with the terms of Rider 1, as soon as practical after the Grant Agreement has received final approval from all necessary parties. The total amount of this grant is $[enter grant amount], and no payments shall be made under this agreement in excess of that amount. At its discretion, the Department may increase or decrease this total grant amount through a revised Miscellaneous Encumbrance as a result of changes in applicable appropriations or allocations or certifications of available funds.

10. This Grant Agreement may be cancelled by the Department, in accordance with Paragraph 18 of Rider 6, upon thirty (30) days prior written notice.

11. This Grant Agreement contains all the terms and conditions agreed on by the parties. Any modifications or waivers of this agreement shall only be valid when they have been reduced to writing, duly signed, and attached to the original of this agreement. No other agreements, oral or otherwise, regarding the subject matter of this agreement, shall be deemed to exist or to bind any of the parties hereto.

Applicants: On the following page, two agency representatives must sign in the Grantee spaces (in blue ink) to bind the applicant agency to the terms and conditions of the grant agreement, should the application be selected for funding. Do not write below the Grantee section. Submit the signature page only as part of the technical portion of the application.

Figure 3–3 *continued*

Grant Agreement   3

IN WITNESS WHEREOF, the parties hereto have caused this Grant Agreement to be executed by its duly authorized officials.

GRANTEE   **GRANTEE**

_____   _____
SIGNATURE   **SIGNATURE**

Print or type name and title: **Print or type name and title:**

_____   _____

COMMONWEALTH OF PENNSYLVANIA
DEPARTMENT OF PUBLIC WELFARE

Program Deputy Secretary   **Secretary**

_____
SIGNATURE   SIGNATURE

COMPTROLLER – DEPARTMENT OF PUBLIC WELFARE
I hereby certify that funds in the amount shown are available under the Appropriation Symbols as shown.

AMOUNT	SOURCE	APPROPRIATION SYMBOL	PROGRAM

_____
SIGNATURE

COMPTROLLER FOR BUDGET SECRETARY

_____
SIGNATURE

Approved as to Legality and Form:

_____	_____	_____
OFFICE OF LEGAL COUNSEL	DEPUTY ATTORNEY GENERAL	DEPUTY GENERAL COUNSEL
DEPARTMENT OF PUBLIC WELFARE	OFFICE OF ATTORNEY GENERAL	OFFICE OF GENERAL COUNSEL
	(when required)	(when required)

Figure 3–3 *continued*

February 2005

U.S. ARMY RESEARCH OFFICE
GENERAL TERMS AND CONDITIONS
FOR GRANT AWARDS TO EDUCATIONAL
INSTITUTIONS AND OTHER NONPROFIT ORGANIZATIONS

TABLE OF CONTENTS

Figure 3–4 *U.S. Army Research Office Grant terms and conditions.*
Source: U.S. Army Research Office.

31. Debarment and Suspension	39. Officials Not to Benefit
32. Termination and Enforcement	40. Retention and Access to Records
33. Program Income	41. Certifications
34. Security	42. Data Collection
35. Representations and Assurances	43. Site Visits
36. Prohibition on Use of Human Subjects	44. International Air Travel
37. Prohibition on Use of Laboratory Animals	45. Cargo Preference
38. Research Involving Recombinant DNA Molecules	46. Military Recruiting on Campus

1. **Acceptance of Grant.** The recipient is not required to countersign the grant document; however, the recipient agrees to the conditions specified in the Research Grant and the Articles contained herein unless notice of disagreement is furnished to the Grants Officer within fifteen (15) calendar days after the date of the Grants Officer's signature. In case of disagreement, the recipient shall not assess the grant any costs of the research unless and until such disagreement(s) is resolved.

2. **Recipient Responsibility.**

   a. The recipient will bear primary responsibility for the conduct of the research and will exercise judgment towards attaining the stated research objectives within the limits of the grant's terms and conditions.

   b. The principal investigator(s) specified in the grant award will be continuously responsible for the conduct of the research project and will be closely involved with the research effort. The principal investigator, operating within the policies of the recipient, is in the best position to determine the means by which the research may be conducted most effectively.

   c. The recipient is the responsible authority, without recourse to the ARO regarding the settlement and satisfaction of all contractual and administrative issues arising out of procurements entered into in support of an award or other agreement.

   d. Recipients are responsible for monitoring each project, program, subaward, function or activity supporting the award. Recipients shall monitor subawards to

Figure 3–4 *continues*

ensure sub recipients have met the audit requirements as delineated in DODGARs §32.26.

3. Order of Precedence. The terms and conditions specified in the Research Grant shall take precedence over these General Terms and Conditions in resolving any inconsistencies or conflicts.

4. Administration and Cost Principles. The following documents and attachments thereto, effective the earlier of (i) the start date of this grant or (ii) the date on which the recipient incurs costs to be assessed the grant, are incorporated by reference as part of this grant:

> a. 2 CFR Part 215 "Uniform Administrative Requirements for Grants and Agreements with Institutions of Higher Education, Hospitals, and Other Nonprofit Organizations."

> b. OMB Circular A-21, "Cost Principles for Educational Institutions."

> c. OMB Circular A-122, "Cost Principles for Nonprofit Organizations."

> d. OMB Circular A-133, "Audits of States, Local Governments, and Nonprofit Organizations."

> e. DOD 3210.6-R, "DoD Grant and Agreement Regulations (DODGARs)."

Note: For those nonprofit organizations specifically exempted from the provisions of OMB Circular A-122, Subpart 31.2 of the Federal Acquisition Regulation (FAR) (48 CFR Subpart 31.2) shall apply.

The above OMB documents may be obtained from:

Executive Office of the President, telephone: (202) 395-3080 or 7250

Office of Management and Budget
725 17th Street, N.W.
Washington, DC 20503

Or http://www.whitehouse.gov/omb/circulars

The DODGARs may be obtained from:

http://www.dtic.mil/whs/directives/corres/html/32106r.htm

5. Standards for Financial Management Systems:

Figure 3–4 *continued*

a. Recipient's financial management systems shall provide for the following:

> 1. Accurate, current and complete disclosure of the financial results of each federally sponsored project or program in accordance with the reporting requirements set forth in DODGARs §32.52.
>
> 2. Records that identify adequately the source and application of funds for federally sponsored activities. These records shall contain information pertaining to Federal awards, authorizations, obligations, unobligated balances, assets, outlays, income and interest.
>
> 3. Effective control over and accountability for all funds, property and other assets. Recipients shall adequately safeguard all such assets and assure they are used solely for authorized purposes.
>
> 4. Comparison of outlays with budget amounts for each award.
>
> 5. Written procedures to minimize the time elapsing between the transfer of funds to the recipient from the U.S. Treasury and the issuance or redemption of checks, warrants or payments by other means for program purposes by the recipient.
>
> 6. Written procedures for determining the reasonableness, allocability and allowability of costs in accordance with the provisions of the applicable Federal cost principles (see DODGARs §32.27) and the terms and conditions of the award.
>
> 7. Accounting records including cost accounting records that are supported by source documentation.

b. Where the Federal Government guarantees or insures the repayment of money borrowed by the recipient, the ARO, at its discretion, may require adequate bonding and insurance if the bonding and insurance requirements of the recipient are not deemed adequate to protect the interest of the Federal Government.

c. The ARO may require adequate fidelity bond coverage where the recipient lacks sufficient coverage to protect the Federal Government's interest.

d. Where bonds are required in the situations described above, the bonds shall be obtained from companies holding certificates of authority as acceptable sureties, as prescribed in 31 CFR part 223, "Surety Companies Doing Business with the United States."

Figure 3–4 *continues*

6. Amendment of the Grant. The only method by which this grant may be amended is by a formal, written amendment signed by the Grants Officer. No other communications, whether oral or in writing, are valid.

7. Waivers of OMB Circular Prior Approvals and Other Authorizations.

a. All prior approvals required by OMB CircularA-21 and A-110 are waived except for the following:

1. Change in the scope or objectives of the research project, the methodology or experiment when such is stated in the grant as a specific objective.

2. Any request for additional funding.

3. Expenditures for equipment costing $5,000 or more not specifically identified in the budget incorporated as part of the grant.

4. Expenditures for foreign travel not specifically identified in the budget incorporated as part of the grant.

5. A change in principal investigator or project director (PI/PD).

6. The continuation of the research work during the absence for more than three (3) months, or a twenty-five (25) percent reduction in time devoted to the project, by the approved PI/PD.

7. Unless described in the application and funded in the approved awards, the subaward, transfer or contracting out of any work under an award. This provision does not apply to the purchase of supplies, material, equipment or general support services.

b. Prior approval is not required to transfer amounts budgeted for indirect costs to absorb increases in direct costs, or vice versa.

c. Prior approval must be requested to initiate a one-time, no-cost extension.

8. Preaward Costs. The recipient may incur Preaward costs in accordance with the DODGARs §32.25(d)(2)(i). Incurring preaward costs more than 90 calendar days prior to award requires the prior approval of the ARO.

9. Unobligated Balances. In the absence of any specific notice to the contrary, the recipient is authorized to carry forward unobligated balances to subsequent

Figure 3–4 *continued*

funding periods of this grant agreement in accordance with DODGARs §32.25(d)(2)(ii).

10. <u>Approval of Change in Performance Period</u>. Extensions of performance periods must be based on a request in writing to the Grants Officer and must be received at least thirty (30) calendar days prior to the end of the current performance period.

11. <u>Payments.</u>

a. Payments to the recipient shall be by the use of a predetermined schedule of payments or reimbursement.

b. Recipients not receiving predetermined scheduled payments shall submit requests for payment using the SF 270, Request for Advance or Reimbursement, no more frequently than monthly. The request shall be submitted to the Office of Naval Research identified in the Research Grant.

c. Payments will be made by the following Government payment office unless specified in the special terms and conditions article of the Research Grant.

Defense Finance and Accounting Service (1-888-332-7742)
Rock Island Operating Location
Building 68
DFAS-RI-FPV
Rock Island, IL 61299-8301

d. Information regarding submission of payment vouchers via the Department of Defense Wide Area Work Flow system will be specified in the special terms and conditions article of the Research Grant.

12. <u>Funding Increments and/or Options</u>. The recipient is advised that the grantor's obligation to provide funding for increments and/or options included in the grant is contingent upon satisfactory performance and the availability of funds. Accordingly, no legal liability on the part of the grantor exists unless or until funds are made available to the grantor and notice of such availability is confirmed in writing to the recipient. Performance of the research must be deemed satisfactory in the judgment of the ARO Scientific Officer/Technical Monitor.

13. <u>Cost Sharing</u>. Unless specified otherwise in the Special Terms and Conditions paragraph of the Research Grant, cost sharing, if any, is included in accordance with 2 CFR Part 215, and DODGARs §32.23.

Figure 3–4 *continues*

14. <u>Allowable Costs.</u>

    a. The allowability of costs incurred by non-profit organizations that may be recipients or subrecipients of awards subject to this part, or contractors under such awards, is determined in accordance with the provisions of OMB Circular A-122, "Cost Principles for Non-Profit Organizations."

    b. The allowability of costs incurred by institutions of higher education that may be recipients, subrecipients, or contractors is determined in accordance with the provisions of OMB Circular A-21, "Cost Principles for Educational Institutions."

    c. Where a funding period is specified, a recipient may charge to the award only allowable costs resulting from obligations incurred during the funding period and any preaward costs authorized by ARO.

15. <u>Program Income</u>.

    a. All program income earned during the project period (except proceeds from the sale of real and personal property and license fees and royalties received as a result of copyrights or patents produced under the grant) shall be retained by the recipient and, deducted from the total project's allowable costs in determining the net allowable costs on which the Federal share of costs will be based.

    b. Unless program regulations or the terms and conditions of the award provide otherwise, recipients shall have no obligation to the Federal Government regarding program income earned after the end of the project period.

    c. Costs incident to the generation of program income may be deducted from gross income to determine program income, provided these costs have not been charged to the award. (See DODGARs §32.24).

16. <u>Interest Earned.</u> Interest earned will be subject to guidelines as specified in DODGARs §32.22.

17. <u>Debt Collection.</u> The establishment of debts owed by recipients of grants and transferring them to payment offices for collection shall be dealt with in accordance with DODGARs §22.820.

18. <u>Audits.</u> Recipients are to periodically have independent, financial and compliance audits subject to DODGARs §32.26.

19. <u>Subawards.</u> Recipients shall flow down requirements to subawards in accordance with DODGARs §32.5.

Figure 3–4 *continued*

20. Procurement Standards. Recipients shall comply with the standards set forth in DODGARs §32.40 through .49 and applicable Federal statutes and Executive Orders when expending Federal funds for supplies, equipment, real property, and expendable property. Upon request, recipients shall make available for the ARO's pre-award review, procurement documents such as requests for proposals or invitations for bids, independent cost estimates, etc. in accordance with DODGARs §32.44 (e).

21. Title to Expendable and Nonexpendable Property. Unless specified otherwise in the Special Terms and Conditions paragraph of the Research Grant, title to all expendable and nonexpendable tangible personal property purchased with grant funds shall be vested in the recipient after acquisition without further obligation to the government to enhance the university infrastructure for future performance of defense research and related, science and engineering education. The ARO shall not reserve the right to transfer title. Such property is considered exempt property and subject to the conditions established in 2 CFR 215 and the DODGARs §32.33. Recipients are to manage property in accordance with DODGARs §32.30 through 32.37.

22. Patent Rights. The clause, "Rights to Inventions Made by Nonprofit Organizations and Small Business Firms Under Government Grants, Contracts and Cooperative Agreements," (37 CFR Part 401), is incorporated as part of the grant by reference. Invention reports shall be filed at least annually and at the end of the grant's performance period. Annual reports are due sixty (60) days after the anniversary date of the grant and final reports are due ninety (90) days after the expiration of the final research period. The recipient shall use DD Form 882, Report of Inventions and Subcontracts, to file the invention reports. Negative reports are required. The grant shall not be closed out until all invention reporting requirements are met.

23. Rights in Technical Data and Computer Software. Rights in technical data and computer software under this grant shall be as described in the DODGARs §32.36.

24. Publication and Acknowledgment. Publication, acknowledgement and disclosure of federal funding under this grant shall be as described in the DODGARs §32.36.

25. Technical Reporting Requirements. For detailed technical reporting requirements and instructions, see ARO Form 18, "Reporting Instructions," found on ARO's website at http://**www.aro.army.mil**

26. Financial Reporting Requirements.

a. The following financial reports are required for recipients receiving funds through a predetermined payment schedule:

Figure 3–4 *continues*

1. Report of Federal Cash Transaction (SF 272) (Quarterly): Due within 15 working days following the end of each quarter.

2. Financial Status Report (SF 269) (Final): Due at completion of grant.

b. The following financial reports are required for recipients receiving funds by reimbursement:

1. Report of Federal Cash Transaction (SF 272): Due annually.

2. Financial Status Report (SF 269) (Final): Due at completion of grant.

c. All reports shall be submitted to the Office of Naval Research Office identified in the Research Grant.

d. Copies of these forms may be found on the internet at

http://www.whitehouse.gov/omb/grants/sf269.pdf

http://www.whitehouse.gov/omb/grants/sf269a.pdf

http://www.whitehouse.gov/omb/grants/sf272.pdf

http://www.whitehouse.gov/omb/grants/sf272a.pdf

27. After-the-Award Requirements. Closeout, subsequent adjustments, continuing responsibilities, and collection of amounts due are subject to requirements found in DODGARs §32.71through 73.

28. Foreign Travel Reporting Requirement. Within thirty (30) days after returning to the United States from foreign travel, the Principal Investigator shall submit an acceptable trip report to the Grants Officer summarizing the highlights of the trip. Reimbursement for travel is contingent upon receipt of an acceptable trip report. If the trip report is not received by the required date, reimbursement will not be authorized.

29. Delegation of Administration Duties. Certain grant administration duties have been delegated to the Office of Naval Research (ONR) identified in the Research Grant. These duties are as follows:

a. Provisionally approve all Requests for Advance or Reimbursement (SF 270).

Figure 3–4 *continued*

b. Perform all property administration services except the approval of recipient's requests to purchase equipment with grant funds. Such approvals must be granted by the ARO Grants Officer.

c. Perform all plant clearance functions.

d. Approve requests for Registration of Scientific and Technical Information Services (DD Form 1540).

e. Obtain the interim (if required) and final financial report(s).

f. Obtain the interim patent report(s).

g. Execute administrative closeout procedures, which includes the following:

> 1. Obtain the final Report of Inventions and Subcontracts (DD Form 882).
>
> 2. Obtain final payment request, if any.
>
> 3. Obtain final property report and dispose of purchased property and government furnished equipment (GFE) in accordance with the DODGARs Part 22, Subpart G.
>
> 4. Perform a review of final incurred costs and assist the Grants Officer in resolving exceptions, if any, resulting from questioned costs.
>
> 5. Assure that all refunds due the Government are received by the grantor.

NOTE: This term and condition is **not applicable** to instrumentation and equipment grant awards.

30. Claims, Disputes and Appeals. Claims, disputes, and appeals shall be processed in accordance with the procedures in DODGARs §22.815.

31. Debarment and Suspension. The ARO and grant recipients shall comply with DODGARs Part 25 which restricts sub awards and contracts with certain parties that are debarred, suspended or otherwise excluded from or ineligible for participation in Federal assistance programs or activities.

32. Termination and Enforcement. Recipients shall be subject to the termination and enforcement conditions found in DODGARs §32.61 and §32.62.

Figure 3–4 *continues*

33. <u>Security</u>. As a general rule, principal investigators will not need access to classified security information in the conduct of research supported under this grant. Should it appear that access to such information is desirable, the recipient shall advise the grantor and request clearance for the investigator. Should information be developed under the course of work under this grant that, in the judgment of the principal investigator or the recipient, should be classified, the Grants Officer shall be notified immediately.

34. <u>Representations and Assurances.</u> By accepting funds under this grant, the recipient assures that it will comply with applicable provisions of the following national policies:

a. National policies prohibiting discrimination:

1. On the basis of race, color, or national origin, in Title VI of the Civil Rights Act of 1964 (42 U.S.C. 2000d, et seq.), as implemented by DoD regulations at 32 CFR Part 195.

2. On the basis of sex or blindness, in Title IX of the Education Amendments of 1972 (20 U.S.C. 1681, et seq.).

3. On the basis of age, in the Age Discrimination Act of 1975 (42 U.S.C. 6101, et seq.), as implemented by Department of Health and Human Services regulations at 45 CFR Part 90.

4. On the basis of handicap, in: Section 504 of the Rehabilitation Act of 1973 (29 U.S.C. 794), as implemented by Department of Justice regulations at 28 CFR Part 41 and DOD regulations at 32 CFR Part 56 and the Architectural Barriers Act of 1968 (42 U.S.C. 4151, et seq.).

b. Environmental Standards:

1. Comply with applicable provisions of the Clean Air Act (42 U.S.C. 7401, et seq.) and Clean Water Act (33 U.S.C. 1251 et seq.), as implemented by Executive Order 11738 [3 CFR, 1971-1975 Comp., p. 799] and Environmental Protection Agency (EPA) rules at 40 CFR Part 15. In accordance with the EPA rules, the recipient further agrees that it will:

(a) Not use any facility on the EPA's List of Violating Facilities in performing any award that is nonexempt under 40 CFR 15.5, as long as the facility remains on the list.

Figure 3–4 *continued*

(b) Notify the awarding agency if it intends to use a facility that is on the List or has been recommended for placement on the List of Violating Facilities.

2. Identify to the awarding agency any impact this award may have on:

(a). The quality of the human environment, and provide help the agency may need to comply with the National Environmental Policy Act (NEPA, at 42 U.S.C. 4321, et seq.) and to prepare Environmental Impact Statements or other required environmental documentation. In such cases, the recipient agrees to take no action that will have an adverse environmental impact (e.g., physical disturbance of a site such as breaking of ground) until the agency provides written notification of compliance with the environmental impact analysis process.

(b) Coastal zones, and provide help the agency may need to comply with the Coastal Zone Management Act of 1972 (16 U.S.C. 1451, et seq.), concerning protection of U.S. coastal resources.

(c) Coastal barriers, and provide help the agency may need to comply with the Coastal Barriers Resources Act (16 U.S.C. 3501 et seq.), concerning preservation of barrier resources.

(d) Any existing or proposed component of the National Wild and Scenic Rivers system, and provide help the agency may need to comply with the wild and Scenic Rivers Act of 1968 (16 U.S.C. 1271, et seq.).

c. Live Organisms:

1. For human subjects, the Common Federal Policy for the Protection of Human Subjects, codified by the Department of Health and Human Services at 45 CFR part 46 and implemented by the Department of Defense at 32 CFR part 219.

2. For animals:

(a) Rules on animal acquisition, transport, care, handling, and use in: (i) 9 CFR parts 1-4, Department of Agriculture rules that implement the Laboratory Animal Welfare Act of 1966 (7 U.S.C. 2131-2156); and (ii)

Figure 3–4 *continues*

the "Guide for the Care and Use of Laboratory Animals," National Institutes of Health Publication No. 86-23.

(b). Rules of the Departments of Interior (50 CFR parts 10-24) and Commerce (50 CFR parts 217-227) implementing laws and conventions on the taking, possession, transport, purchase, sale, export, or import of wildlife and plants, including the: Endangered Species Act of 1973 (16 U.S.C. 1531-1543); Marine Mammal Protection Act (16 U.S.C. 1361-1384); Lacey Act (18 U.S.C. 42); and Convention on International Trade in Endangered Species of Wild Fauna and Flora.

35. Prohibition on Use of Human Subjects. Notwithstanding any other provisions contained in this grant or incorporated by reference herein, the recipient is expressly forbidden to use or subcontract or subgrant for the use of human subjects in any manner whatsoever without the express written approval from the Grants Officer.

36. Prohibition on Use of Laboratory Animals. Notwithstanding any other provisions contained in this grant or incorporated by reference herein, the recipient is expressly forbidden to use or subcontract or subgrant for the use of laboratory animals in any manner whatsoever without the express written approval of the Grants Officer.

37. Research Involving Recombinant DNA Molecules. Any recipient performing research involving recombinant DNA molecules and/or organisms and viruses containing recombinant DNA molecules agrees by acceptance of this award to comply with the National Institutes of Health "Guidelines for Research Involving Recombinant DNA Molecules, " July 5, 1994 (59 FR34496) amended August 5, 1994 (59 FR40170) amended April 27, 1995 (60 FR 20726), or such later revision of those guidelines as may be published in the Federal Register.

38. Officials Not to Benefit. No member of or delegate to Congress, or resident commissioner, shall be admitted to any share or part of this agreement, or to any benefit arising from it, in accordance with 41 U.S.C. 22.

39. Retention and Access to Records. Retention and access to records pertinent to this award are subject to the requirements of DODGARs §32.53.

40. Certifications. By accepting funds under this agreement, the recipient acknowledges the following:

a. 32 CFR Part 25 regarding debarment, suspension, and other responsibility matters.

b. 32 CFR Part 26 regarding drug-free workplace requirements.

c. Certification at appendix A to 32 CFR Part 28 regarding lobbying.

Figure 3–4 *continued*

41. <u>Data Collection</u>. Data collection activities, if any, performed under this grant are the responsibility of the recipient. Awarding agency support of the project does not constitute approval of the survey design, questionnaire content, or data collection procedures. The recipient shall not represent to respondents that such data are being collected for or in association with the awarding agency without the specific written approval of the cognizant awarding agency official. However, this requirement is not intended to preclude mention of the awarding agency support of the project in response to an inquiry or acknowledgment of such support in any publication of this data.

42. <u>Site Visits</u>. The grantor, through authorized representatives, has the right, at all reasonable times, to make site visits to review project accomplishments and to provide such technical assistance as may be required. The recipient shall provide, and shall require its sub recipients and subcontractors to provide all reasonable facilities and assistance for the safety and convenience of the government representatives in the performance of site visits. All site visits and evaluations shall be performed in a manner that does not unduly interfere with or delay the work.

43. <u>International Air Travel.</u> Travel supported by U.S. Government funds under this agreement shall use U.S.-flag air carriers (air carriers holding certificates under 49 U.S.C. 41102) for international air transportation of people and property to the extent that such service is available, in accordance with the International Air Transportation Fair Competitive Practices Act of 1974 (49 U.S.C. 40118) and the interpretative guidelines issued by the Comptroller General of the United States in the March 31, 1981, amendment to Comptroller General Decision B138942.

44. <u>Cargo Preference</u>. The recipient agrees that it will comply with the Cargo Preference Act of 1954 (46 U.S.C. 1241), as implemented by Department of Transportation regulations at 46 CFR 381.7, which requires that at least 50 percent of equipment, materials or commodities procured or otherwise obtained with U.S. Government funds under this agreement, and which may be transported by ocean vessel, shall be transported on privately owned U.S.-flag commercial vessels, if available.

45. <u>Military Recruiting on Campus</u>. Military recruiting on campus under this award shall be as specified in the DODGARs §22.520, Military Recruiting and Reserve Officer Training Corps Program Access to Institutions of Higher Education, which is incorporated by reference.

Figure 3–4 *continued*

South Dakota Department of Tourism and State Development

South Dakota Arts Council
711 E. Wells Avenue
Pierre, SD 57501-3369

PLEASE NOTE: <u>This document MUST be signed and returned along with your Touring Arts Grant Agreement and W-9 to the South Dakota Arts Council office.</u> (Please keep a file copy of this document.)

TOURING ARTIST GRANT TERMS AND CONDITIONS

CREDIT

All published material and announcements regarding any project or production which is financed in part under this grant must include the following special acknowledgment statement: *South Dakota Arts Council support is provided with funds from the State of South Dakota, through the Department of Tourism and State Development, and the National Endowment for the Arts.* (In order to inform audiences of the importance of governmental support for the arts, we request that you include a display advertisement in your printed programs and/or organizational newsletters. Camera-ready slicks for this purpose are provided for you.)

FINANCIAL MANAGEMENT

- Grants are for the period specified in the approved application. Funds must be obligated within the period stated unless an extension has been approved by the South Dakota Arts Council.

- Funds granted shall be expended solely for the activities described in the approved application unless specific changes have been approved by the South Dakota Arts Council. Any funds granted but not expended or committed shall be returned to the South Dakota Arts Council at the conclusion of the grant period.

- The applicant assures that fund accounting, auditing and monitoring and such evaluation procedures as may be necessary to keep such records as the South Dakota Arts Council shall prescribe will be provided to assure fiscal control, proper management, and efficient disbursement of funds received through the South Dakota Arts Council. In accordance with 34 CFR 80.21(c), grantees/subgrantees shall be paid in advance, provided they maintain and demonstrate the willingness and ability to maintain procedures to minimize the time elapsing between the transfer of the funds and their disbursement by the grantee and subgrantee. **The funds should be requested when they can be expended within a 30-60 day time period.**

- Grantees shall establish and maintain accounts in such a manner as to separate grant funds and matching funds and shall reflect all receipts, obligations and disbursements of project funds. Since expenditures of these funds are subject to audit, all financial records, including substantiating documentation (e.g. payroll vouchers, invoices, bills) must be maintained for three years or until a federal audit has been completed and any questions arising from it have been resolved, whichever is the lesser period.

Figure 3–5 *South Dakota Arts Council Touring Artists terms and conditions.*
Source: Reprinted with permission of the South Dakota Arts Council.

Grant Terms and Conditions (Certified Assurances)
Touring Arts Grantees
Page 2

Grants made by the National Endowment for the Arts and sub-granted by the South Dakota Arts Council are subject to the requirements outlined in OMB Circulars A-21, A-87, A-110, and A-122. Grantees agree to abide by all federal and state regulations, including the following certified assurances.

CERTIFIED ASSURANCES

1. **Fair Labor Standards Act** states that all professional performers and related or supporting personnel employed on projects or productions which are financed in whole or in part under the grant shall receive not less than the minimum compensation as determined by the Secretary of Labor.

No part of any project or production which is financed in whole or in part under the grant will be performed or engaged in under working conditions which are unsanitary or hazardous or dangerous to the health and safety of the employees engaged in such project or production.

2. **Title VI of the Civil Rights Act of 1964**, as amended, provides that no person in the United States shall, *on the grounds of race, color or national origin*, be excluded from participation in, be denied benefits of, or be subject to discrimination under any program or activity receiving federal financial assistance. Title VI also extends protection to persons with limited English proficiency.

3. **Section 504 of the Rehabilitation Act of 1973** provides that no otherwise qualified disabled individual in the United States, as defined in section 7(6)*, shall, *solely by reason of his/her disability*, be excluded from the participation in, be denied the benefits of, or be subjected to discrimination under any program or activity receiving federal assistance. Under this regulation, a federally funded arts program when viewed in its entirety must be accessible to all persons. The National Endowment for the Arts issued its regulations in 1979 to enforce the existing law. Failure to comply with Section 504 can result in loss of federal funds.

* For the purpose of Section 504, the term "disabled individual" means any person who (a) has a physical or mental impairment which substantially limits one or more of such person's major life activities, (b) has a record of such impairment, or (c) is regarded as having such an impairment.

A self-evaluation must be on file at your organization. The National Endowment for the Arts has developed a Program Evaluation Workbook which may be used by a recipient to conduct a self-evaluation to determine if it is in compliance with 504 requirements. If you have not previously conducted this self-evaluation, you may wish to request a copy of the Program Evaluation Workbook, free of charge, by contacting the South Dakota Arts Council, 800 Governors Drive, Pierre, SD 57501.

4. **Americans with Disabilities Act (*ADA*) of 1990** prohibits discrimination on the basis of disability in employment (Title I), State and Local Government Services (Title II), and places of public accommodation and commercial facilities (Title III).

5. **Age Discrimination Act of 1975** provides that no person in the United States shall, *on the basis of age*, be excluded from participation in, be denied the benefits of, or be subject to discrimination under any program or activity receiving federal financial assistance.

6. **Title IX of the Education Amendments of 1972** provides that no person in the United States shall, *on the basis of sex*, be excluded from participation in, be denied the benefits of, or be subjected to discrimination under any program or activity receiving federal assistance.

Figure 3–5 *continues*

Grant Terms and Conditions (Certified Assurances)
Touring Arts Grantees
Page 3

7. **Drug Free Workplace Act of 1988** requires that local educational agencies adopt a Drug Free Workplace Policy which is in compliance with the Drug Free Workplace Act and that grantees with more than ten employees identify a coordinator to implement the provisions of this act.

8. **Pro-Children Act of 1994** requires that smoking not be permitted in any indoor facility used routinely or regularly for the provision of "children's services" to persons under age 18, if the services are funded by specified federal programs either directly or through state or local governments. Local educational agencies must adopt the provisions of this act.

9. **Gun Free Schools Act** requires that local educational agencies adopt a Gun Free Policy, which is in compliance with SDCL 13-32-4.

10. As required by **Section 1352, Title 31 of the US Code**, grantees must adhere to the **prohibition against lobbying** within a federally supported grant project which states that no federal appropriated funds have been paid or will be paid by or on behalf of the grantee, to any person for influencing or attempting to influence an officer or employee of any agency, a member of Congress, an officer or employee of Congress, or an employee of a member of Congress in connection with the making of any federal grant, the entering into any federal grant or cooperative agreement, and the extension, continuation, renewal, amendment, or modification of any federal grant or cooperative agreement.

11. As required by **Executive Order 12549, Debarment and Suspension**, the Grantee certifies that it and its principals:
    (1) Are not presently debarred, suspended, proposed for debarment, declared ineligible, or voluntarily excluded from covered transactions by any federal department or agency;
    (2) Have not within a three-year period preceding the awarding of this grant been convicted of or had a civil judgment rendered against them for commission of fraud or a criminal offense in connection with obtaining, attempting to obtain, or performing a public (federal, state, or local) transaction or contract under a public transaction; violation of federal or state antitrust statutes or commission of embezzlement, theft, forgery, bribery, falsifications or destruction of records, making false statements, or receiving stolen property.
    (3) Are not presently indicted for or otherwise criminally or civilly charged by a governmental agency (federal, state, or local) with commission of any of the offenses enumerated in paragraph (11)(2) of this document;
    (4) Have not within a three-year period preceding this grant award had one or more public transactions (federal, state, or local) terminated for cause or default.
    Where the Grantee is unable to certify any of the above statements, he or she shall send a written explanation to the South Dakota Arts Council.

12. **The Native American Graves Protection and Repatriation Act of 1990** (25 U.S.C. 3001 et seq.) applies to any organization which controls or possesses Native American human remains and associated funerary objects, and which receives Federal funding, even for a purpose unrelated to the Act.

13. As required by **Federal Debt Status** (OMB Circular A-120), the grantee certifies that it is not delinquent in the repayment of any Federal debt.

14. All **travel outside the United States**, its territories, and Canada must be approved in writing by the State Arts Council before travel is undertaken. Additionally, any foreign air travel (inclusive of persons or property) that is paid in whole or in part with Endowment funds must be performed on a U.S. air carrier or a foreign air carrier under an air transport agreement with the United States when these services are available. U.S. air-carrier service is considered available even though a comparable or different kind of service can be provided at less cost by a foreign air carrier and/or foreign air-carrier service is preferred by, or is more convenient for, the traveler. For additional guidance, please contact the South Dakota Arts Council.

Figure 3–5 *continued*

Grant Terms and Conditions (Certified Assurances)
Touring Arts Grantees
Page 4

15. Consistent with 41 U.S.C. 10a-10c, "**Buy American Act**," subgrantees who are purchasing equipment and products through an Endowment-supported grant are encouraged, whenever possible, to purchase American-made equipment and products.

16. If your non-profit organization receives **$300,000 or more in federal financial assistance**, the State of South Dakota requires that an annual audit be conducted in accordance with OMB Circular A-133. Audits shall be completed and filed with the Department of Legislative Audit within the earlier of 30 days after the receipt of the auditor's report(s), or nine months after end of the audit period.*

*   Audits must be conducted by an auditor that is approved by the Auditor General of the State of South Dakota. Auditor approval must be obtained annually and can be requested by forwarding a copy of the audit engagement letter to the Department of Legislative Audit. The Department of Legislative Audit will notify each auditor of approval or disapproval. For information concerning audits, contact: **Department of Legislative Audit, A-133 Coordinator, 427 S. Chapelle, c/o 500 E. Capitol, Pierre, SD 57501**

17. Recipients must maintain financial records, supporting documents, statistical records, and all other records pertinent to an award consistent with the provisions outlined in OMB Circular A-110, Section 53 or the Common Rule, Section 1157.42 as applicable. Generally, the retention period is three years from the date the final financial status report is filed.

18. The applicant assures that fund accounting, auditing, and monitoring and such evaluation procedures as may be necessary to keep such records as the South Dakota Arts Council shall prescribe will be provided to assure fiscal control, proper management, and efficient disbursement of funds received through the South Dakota Arts Council. In accordance with 34 CFR 80.21(c), Grantees/subgrantees shall be paid in advance, provided they maintain and demonstrate the willingness and ability to maintain procedures to minimize the time elapsing between the transfer of the funds and their disbursement by the grantee and subgrantee. **The funds should be requested when they can be expended within a 30-60 day time period.**

As the Grantee's authorized representative, I certify that _____
(Name of Grantee)
is in compliance with the GRANT TERMS AND CONDITIONS and CERTIFIED ASSURANCES outlined in this document.

Name (please print or type): _____

Title (please print or type). _____

Signature: _____   Date: _____

THIS DOCUMENT (1) must be completed and returned together with signed copies of (2) THE W-9 FORM AND (3) the GRANT CONTRACT & REQUEST FOR PAYMENT form if you represent an organization OR with the GRANT CONTRACT AGREEMENT if you are on the Touring Arts Roster. Your grant award will not be processed until these documents are on file in our office.

Figure 3–5 *continued*

RSVP
Standard Grant Terms and Conditions
[Revised 9/25/2006]

[These standard terms and condition are subject to change. The standard terms and conditions that apply to a particular Notice of Grant Award (NGA) are provided as part of the NGA. Special terms and conditions may also apply to a particular award.]

Interest Bearing Account Must Maintain Advance Federal Funds
Institutions of higher education and other non-profit organizations covered by OMB Circular A-110 must maintain advance Federal funds in an interest bearing account. Interest earned on advances deposited in such accounts shall be remitted annually in a check, made payable to the U.S. Treasury, to the Department of Health and Human Services, Payment Management System, P.O. Box 6021, Rockville, MD 20852. The document transmitting the check must indicate that the payment is interest earned on advanced Federal funds. Interest up to $250 per year may be retained by the grantee for administrative expenses.

Recognition Events
Grantee will assure that at Recognition events, the Corporation is acknowledged as the Federal agency responsible for the primary Federal funding of the project.

Lobby Disclosure
For grant awards exceeding $100,000, pursuant to 31 U.S.C. 1352, the Grantee is required to file a disclosure report, Standard Form LLL, Disclosure of Lobbying Activities, at the end of any quarter, when the Grantee has paid or agreed to pay any lobbying entity for influencing or attempting to influence an officer or employee of any agency, a Member of Congress, an officer or employee of Congress, or an employee of a Member of Congress in connection with a covered Federal action. The report must be submitted to the Corporation State Program Director.

External Evaluation And Data Collection
The grantee must cooperate with the Corporation and its evaluators in all monitoring and evaluation efforts. As part of this effort, the grantee must collect and submit certain project data, as defined in the Project Profile and Volunteer Activity (PPVA) and must provide data as requested or needed to support external evaluations.

Grant Period
Unless otherwise specified, the Grant covers a three year project period. In approving a multiyear project period the Corporation makes an initial award for the first budget period. Additional funding for subsequent budget periods is contingent upon satisfactory progress and the availability of funds. The project period and the budget are noted on the award document.

Financial Status Reports/Jan to Jun and Jul to Dec
Grantees paid through HHS/PMS must submit the Standard Form 269, Financial Status Report (FSR), semi-annually from the start date of the grant to report the status of all funds. FSRs must report expenses on a cumulative basis over the performance period of the grant and be submitted according to the following schedule:

> *Period Covering: Report Due:*
> January 1 to June 30 August 1
> July 1 to December 31 February 1

Programs completing the final year of their grant must submit a final FSR that is cumulative over the entire grant period. This FSR is due 90 days after the close of the grant.

Figure 3–6 *Retired and Senior Volunteer Program standard grant terms and conditions.*
Source: *Corporation of National and Community Service.*

Financial Status Reports/Apr to Sep and Oct to Mar
Grantees paid through HHS/PMS must submit the Standard Form 269, Financial Status Report (FSR), semi-annually from the start date of the grant to report the status of all funds. FSRs must report expenses on a cumulative basis over the performance period of the grant and be submitted according to the following schedule:

> *Period Covering: Report Due:*
> April 1 - September 30 November 1
> October 1 - March 30 May 1

Programs completing the final year of their grant must submit a final FSR that is cumulative over the entire grant period. This FSR is due 90 days after the close of the grant.

SF272 Reporting
Grantees paid through HHS/PMS will report quarterly disbursements to HHS through SMARTLINK II. Grantees will report disbursements using the web based version of the Standard Form 272, Federal Cash Transaction Report, no later than 45 calendar days following the end of each quarter.

Recognition of Federal Funding
When issuing statements, press releases, requests for proposals, bid solicitations, annual reports and other documents describing projects or programs funded in whole or in part with Federal Corporation money, the grantee receiving federal funds, including but not limited to the state and local governments, shall clearly state (1) the percentage of the total cost of the program which will be financed with the Federal Corporation money, and (2) the dollar amount of Federal Corporation funds for the project or program.

Program/Project Manager Authority
The Program/Project Manager for this grant is listed on the face page of the Notice of Grant Award. The Program/Project Manager has full authority to represent the Corporation in connection with management of the technical and programmatic performance of the grant. They are not authorized to change the terms and conditions, estimated costs, or period of performance, or to give approvals, written or verbal, specifically reserved for the grant officer.

Figure 3–6 *continued*

REVISION OF THE NATIONAL SCIENCE FOUNDATION (NSF)
GRANT GENERAL CONDITIONS (GC-1)
June 15th, 2005

Effective June 15th, 2005, new NSF grants and funding amendments to existing NSF grants[1] will begin referencing and are subject to the Grant General Conditions (GC-1) dated 06/15/05. The complete text of the GC-1 (as well as other NSF grant policy issuances) is available electronically on the NSF website.[2]

A comprehensive summary of the significant changes is included below. Any questions regarding these changes may be directed to the Policy Office, Division of Institution and Award Support, on (703) 292-8243 or by e-mail to policy@nsf.gov.

Significant Changes to the Grant General Conditions (GC-1) Dated 6/15/05

♦   **Overall document** has been completely revised to reflect incorporation of the Office of Management and Budget (OMB) Circular A-110 into 2 CFR §215. As a result, references to A-110 sections have been updated thoughout. The document has also been changed to replace the term "awardee" with the term "grantee."

♦   **Prior Approval Requirements, Article 2,** has been supplemented to indicate that prior approval requests must be submitted electronically via FastLane, unless other arrangements have been made in advance with the cognizant NSF Grants Officer.

♦   **Equipment, Article 6,** has been revised and reorganized to consolidate information on inventory requirements into a new section of the Article. Because of increasing threats to information technology systems, the Article also reminds grantees that they must adequately maintain and insure adequate safeguards against the loss, damage, or theft of information technology equipment and systems purchased with NSF funds.

♦   **Significant Project Changes, Article 8,** has been updated to show that the grantee is responsible for maintaining documentation on all subawards and making such documentation available to NSF upon request. Grantees should include descriptions of subaward activities in their annual and final project reports. If the grantee issues subawards exceeding $2,000 for construction, alteration or repair that

---

[1] The NSF Grant General Conditions do not apply to organizations participating in the Federal Demonstration Partnership.
[2] The Policy Office website address is: http://www.nsf.gov/bfa/dias/policy/

Figure 3–7 *National Science Foundation grant terms and conditions revisions.*
Source: National Science Foundation.

Significant Changes
Page 2

are within the scope of 2 CFR §215 Appendix A, appropriate clauses should be included in the applicable subawards.

♦　　　**Travel, Article 10,** has been modified to state that, except as provided in the governing cost principles, the difference between economy airfare and a higher-class airfare is unallowable.

♦　　　**Project Reporting Requirements, Article 15 and Expenditure Reports, Article 16,** are now 2 new distinct Articles that contain information on NSF reporting requirements. Information on annual and final project reporting requirements have been consolidated into Article 15 and information on expenditure reports has now been moved to a separate Article 16. The content of the Articles has not changed except that language has been added to Article 15 with regard to submission of special reports.

♦　　　**Publications, Article 20,** has been updated to reflect that the grantee is responsible for ensuring that the cognizant NSF Program Officer is provided access, either electronically or in paper form, to a copy of every publication of material based on or developed under an award.

♦　　　**Patent Rights, Article 21,** has been supplemented to include the full text of the Patent Rights clause that was previously only contained in the NSF Grant Policy Manual.

♦　　　**Nondiscrimination, Article 27,** has been modified to include additional sections of Title IX of the Education Amendments of 1972 that are applicable to NSF awards.

♦　　　**National Security: Classifiable Results Originating Under NSF Grants, Article 28,** has been modified to show that Executive Order (E.O.) 12958 has been amended.

♦　　　**Debarment and Suspension, Article 35,** is an entirely new Article that informs recipients that they must fully comply with the requirements stipulated in Subpart C of 45 CFR §620, entitled *"Responsibilities of Participants Regarding Transactions."*

♦　　　**Government Permits and Activities Abroad, Article 39,** has been supplemented to highlight for grantees potential areas of concern with regard to conducting activities abroad.

Figure 3–7 *continued*

REQUEST FOR ADVANCE OR REIMBURSEMENT	OMB APPROVAL NO. 0348-0004		PAGE	OF PAGES

REQUEST FOR ADVANCE OR REIMBURSEMENT

(See instructions on back)

	OMB APPROVAL NO. 0348-0004		PAGE	OF PAGES
1. TYPE OF PAYMENT REQUESTED	a. "X" one or both boxes ☐ ADVANCE ☐ REIMBURSEMENT		2. BASIS OF REQUEST ☐ CASH	
	b. "X" the applicable box ☐ FINAL ☐ PARTIAL		☐ ACCRUAL	

3. FEDERAL SPONSORING AGENCY AND ORGANIZATIONAL ELEMENT TO WHICH THIS REPORT IS SUBMITTED	4. FEDERAL GRANT OR OTHER IDENTIFYING NUMBER ASSIGNED BY FEDERAL AGENCY	5. PARTIAL PAYMENT REQUEST NUMBER FOR THIS REQUEST

6. EMPLOYER IDENTIFICATION NUMBER	7. RECIPIENT'S ACCOUNT NUMBER OR IDENTIFYING NUMBER	8. PERIOD COVERED BY THIS REQUEST	
		FROM *(month, day, year)*	TO *(month, day, year)*

9. RECIPIENT ORGANIZATION	10. PAYEE *(Where check is to be sent if different than item 9)*
Name:	Name:
Number and Street:	Number and Street:
City, State and ZIP Code:	City, State and ZIP Code:

11. COMPUTATION OF AMOUNT OF REIMBURSEMENTS/ADVANCES REQUESTED

PROGRAMS/FUNCTIONS/ACTIVITIES ▶	(a)	(b)	(c)	TOTAL
a. Total program outlays to date *(As of date)*	$	$	$	$ 0.00
b. *Less:* Cumulative program income				0.00
c. Net program outlays *(Line a minus line b)*	0.00	0.00	0.00	0.00
d. Estimated net cash outlays for advance period				0.00
e. Total *(Sum of lines c & d)*	0.00	0.00	0.00	0.00
f. Non-Federal share of amount on line e				0.00
g. Federal share of amount on line e				0.00
h. Federal payments previously requested				0.00
i. Federal share now requested *(Line g minus line h)*	0.00	0.00	0.00	0.00
j. Advances required by month, when requested by Federal grantor agency for use in making prescheduled advances	1st month			0.00
	2nd month			0.00
	3rd month			0.00

12. ALTERNATE COMPUTATION FOR ADVANCES ONLY

a. Estimated Federal cash outlays that will be made during period covered by the advance	$
b. *Less:* Estimated balance of Federal cash on hand as of beginning of advance period	
c. Amount requested *(Line a minus line b)*	$ 0.00

AUTHORIZED FOR LOCAL REPRODUCTION   *(Continued on Reverse)*   STANDARD FORM 270 (Rev. 7-97)
Prescribed by OMB Circulars A-102 and A-110

Figure 3–8 *Request for Advancement or Reimbursement form.*
Source: U.S. Government.

13.	CERTIFICATION		
I certify that to the best of my knowledge and belief the data on the reverse are correct and that all outlays were made in accordance with the grant conditions or other agreement and that payment is due and has not been previously requested.	SIGNATURE OR AUTHORIZED CERTIFYING OFFICIAL		DATE REQUEST SUBMITTED March 24, 2009
	TYPED OR PRINTED NAME AND TITLE		TELEPHONE (AREA CODE, NUMBER, EXTENSION)

This space for agency use

Public reporting burden for this collection of information is estimated to average 60 minutes per response, including time for reviewing instructions, searching existing data sources, gathering and maintaining the data needed, and completing and reviewing the collection of information. Send comments regarding the burden estimate or any other aspect of this collection of information, including suggestions for reducing this burden, to the Office of Management and Budget, Paperwork Reduction Project (0348-0004), Washington, DC 20503.

PLEASE DO NOT RETURN YOUR COMPLETED FORM TO THE OFFICE OF MANAGEMENT AND BUDGET. SEND IT TO THE ADDRESS PROVIDED BY THE SPONSORING AGENCY.

INSTRUCTIONS

Please type or print legibly. Items 1, 3, 5, 9, 10, 11e, 11f, 11g, 11i, 12 and 13 are self-explanatory; specific instructions for other items are as follows:

Item	Entry

2 Indicate whether request is prepared on cash or accrued expenditure basis. All requests for advances shall be prepared on a cash basis.

4 Enter the Federal grant number, or other identifying number assigned by the Federal sponsoring agency. If the advance or reimbursement is for more than one grant or other agreement, insert N/A; then, show the aggregate amounts. On a separate sheet, list each grant or agreement number and the Federal share of outlays made against the grant or agreement.

6 Enter the employer identification number assigned by the U.S. Internal Revenue Service, or the FICE (institution) code if requested by the Federal agency.

7 This space is reserved for an account number or other identifying number that may be assigned by the recipient.

8 Enter the month, day, and year for the beginning and ending of the period covered in this request. If the request is for an advance or for both an advance and reimbursement, show the period that the advance will cover. If the request is for reimbursement, show the period for which the reimbursement is requested.

Note: The Federal sponsoring agencies have the option of requiring recipients to complete items 11 or 12, but not both. Item 12 should be used when only a minimum amount of information is needed to make an advance and outlay information contained in item 11 can be obtained in a timely manner from other reports.

11 The purpose of the vertical columns (a), (b), and (c) is to provide space for separate cost breakdowns when a project has been planned and budgeted by program, function, or

activity. If additional columns are needed, use as many additional forms as needed and indicate page number in space provided in upper right; however, the summary totals of all programs, functions, or activities should be shown in the "total" column on the first page.

11a Enter in "as of date," the month, day, and year of the ending of the accounting period to which this amount applies. Enter program outlays to date (net of refunds, rebates, and discounts), in the appropriate columns. For requests prepared on a cash basis, outlays are the sum of actual cash disbursements for goods and services, the amount of indirect expenses charged, the value of in-kind contributions applied, and the amount of cash advances and payments made to subcontractors and subrecipients. For requests prepared on an accrued expenditure basis, outlays are the sum of the actual cash disbursements, the amount of indirect expenses incurred, and the net increase (or decrease) in the amounts owed by the recipient for goods and other property received and for services performed by employees, contracts, subgrantees and other payees.

11b Enter the cumulative cash income received to date, if requests are prepared on a cash basis. For requests prepared on an accrued expenditure basis, enter the cumulative income earned to date. Under either basis, enter only the amount applicable to program income that was required to be used for the project or program by the terms of the grant or other agreement.

11d Only when making requests for advance payments, enter the total estimated amount of cash outlays that will be made during the period covered by the advance.

13 Complete the certification before submitting this request.

STANDARD FORM 270 (Rev. 7-97) Back

Figure 3–8 *continued*

After accepting the grant award, it is advisable to schedule a meeting with all of the staff and stakeholders associated with the project, review the grants management responsibilities, and begin the implementation process.

Chapter Summary

It is not uncommon for funders to offer a lesser dollar amount than was requested in the proposal. Applicants have to carefully weigh all of the ramifications of accepting less money and how this will impact the project in the areas of methodology, budget, personnel, or evaluation.

A designated individual should be given the authority to accept grant awards and review acceptance paperwork carefully before responding positively. Accepting the grant award actually signals the beginning of the grants management process of a funded project.

Chapter 4

Coordinating Grants Management Tasks

To make the grants management process easier, it helps to coordinate all of the tasks related to management. This is especially critical if a grantee has several grants with overlapping project periods, which usually results in multiple reports due with the same deadline. Grants management will involve several individuals including project staff and director, the finance office, the project evaluator, and in some cases, the chief administrator of the grantee organization. Planning and preparing for grants management early in the process should help make it easier.

Creating a Grant File

A file should be created for each proposal that is funded. Grantees may want to keep an electronic file of scanned documents and a hard copy file as backup. The file should contain the following:

- A copy of the funded proposal
- Regulations for the grant program (usually for a federal grant)
- The award notice received from the funder
- Documents showing any approved revisions or changes to the proposal that was submitted
- Assurances (usually for a federal grant)

- The project budget
- Any correspondence with the funder related to the project
- Memorandums of understanding with collaborative partners in the project
- Records of expenditures, receipts, and purchase orders
- Programmatic, financial, evaluation, and audit reports

Figure 4–1 is the suggested documentation list for recipients of Universal Services Administrative Fund. The Schools and Libraries Program of the Universal Service Fund makes discounts available to eligible schools and libraries for telecommunication services, Internet access, and internal connections. The program is intended to ensure that schools and libraries have access to affordable telecommunications and information services.

Coordination with Project Staff

If a project includes staff that must be hired, the grantee should create all of the needed advertisement for the positions that will be created and funded through the grant. Consulting contracts should also be discussed with the appropriate individuals and prepared in advance.

As soon as the grantee has received official notice of the grant award, the positions should be advertised and staff should be hired as quickly as possible. A meeting of all project staff should be held as soon as they are all in place. Copies of the funded proposal and any alterations to it should be distributed to all staff members. The tasks outlined in the proposal should be reviewed, as should the terms and conditions of the grant.

Decisions should be made regarding who is responsible for specific tasks, and if needed, a responsibility chart can be developed for all staff to refer to during the project implementation. The information included on the chart can include completion of progress reports, evaluation activities and the tools that will be used, monitoring visit dates if known, completion of financial reports, filing requests for project extensions if needed, maintaining programmatic records and financial accounts, purchasing project equipment, inventory control, maintaining records of matching funds, and closing out the grant (discussed in Chapter 9).

For those grantees with multiple, simultaneous grants, a review schedule may be a helpful tool. The schedule can be created to list monthly activities such as reviewing progress of the projects, expenditures for each grant, matching funds received for the grants, and reporting deadlines. By using this type of schedule, it will be easier to monitor all of the grants-related activity within the organization.

Some funders will require that the project director and a staff member attend a conference or training session during the project period. If dates are available, they should be added to the project calendar, as attendance for these is often mandatory and the associated costs are already in the project budget.

UNIVERSAL SERVICES ADMINISTRATIVE FUND
SCHOOLS & LIBRARIES
DOCUMENTATION CHECKLIST

SUGGESTED DOCUMENTATION REQUIREMENT	Completed
I. TECHNOLOGY PLAN	
1. Clear goals and a realistic strategy for using telecommunications and information technology to improve education and library services. The Plan should cover the dates of the funding year and include E-rate funded equipment and services, as well as equipment and services necessary to support E-rate funded equipment and services.	
2. An assessment of the telecommunication services, hardware, software, and other services that will be needed to improve education or library services.	
3. A professional technical development strategy to ensure beneficiary (school or library) staff know how to utilize these E-rate and supporting technologies to improve education or library services.	
4. A technology budget covering the amounts necessary to acquire and support the non-discounted elements of the Technology Plan, e.g., hardware, software, professional development, and other services necessary to implement both the technology and development strategies.	
5. An evaluation process that enables the school(s) or library(ies) to monitor progress in achieving specified Technology Plan goals and objectives, as well as the implementation of changes or corrections to the Technology Plan strategy in response to new developments and opportunities as they arise.	
II. PROGRAM COMPLIANCE	

1. If receiving discounted services from the service provider, maintain copies of the following:
 	
  a. Vendor invoice or reconciliation worksheet (supported by vendor invoices) supporting billing/payment for the undiscounted portion of the E-rate expenditure.
  b. Proof of payment for the undiscounted portion (e.g., cancelled check).
  c. Supporting documentation sufficient to evidence that what was approved per the Funding Commitment Letter was actually procured.
  d. If feasible and obtainable, copies of the invoice submitted by the service	

(continues)

Figure 4–1 *Documentation list for recipients of Universal Service Fund Schools and Libraries support.*
Source: Universal Service Administrative Company.

SUGGESTED DOCUMENTATION REQUIREMENT	Completed
provider to the Schools and Libraries Division and supporting invoice or reconciliation worksheet (obtained from the service provider) supporting the E-rate reimbursement for the beneficiary.	
2. For each Billed Entity Applicant Reimbursement ("BEAR") form submitted to and reimbursed by SLD, maintain copies of the following: a. Vendor invoice or reconciliation worksheet supporting the claim submitted to SLD. b. Proof of payment (e.g., cancelled check) for the total E-rate eligible amount (discounted and non-discounted portion) paid to the service provider. c. Documentation verifying reimbursements as a result of the BEAR form have been received from the service provider and deposited (i.e., copy of remittance advice or vendor payment, bank statements, etc.). d. Copies of any written communication with the vendor concerning attempts to get reimbursements.	
3. Reconciliation of the discounted (based on the approved percentage per the Funding Commitment Decision Letter) and non-discounted portion to equal 100% of the E-rate eligible and funded equipment and/or services cost.	
4. If E-rate eligible service and/or installation or equipment costs are included as part of a larger contract or service/equipment billing, support for the allocation of E-rate eligible amounts and reconciliation of that total to the total amount billed to the beneficiary by the service provider.	
5. If E-rate eligible services or equipment provided by a single service provider are allocated to multiple units (schools or libraries), support for the allocation reconciled to the amounts and locations identified in the approved Application (Form 471).	
6. For internal connections equipment purchased with E-rate funds maintain: a. An Asset Register or other appropriate asset listing which documents the make, model serial number, purchase date and specific location of each item of E-rate funded equipment. b. A Replacement Log reflecting the replacement or upgrading of any E-rate funded equipment.	
7. Proof that all E-rate funded internal connections have been received and installed by the cut-off date (i.e., service provider sign-off, dated test data results, etc.).	
8. Proof that E-rate funded services were provided within the allowable contract period/Funding Year.	

Figure 4–1 *continued*

SUGGESTED DOCUMENTATION REQUIREMENT	Completed
III. CONTRACTS	
1. Copies of all signed and executed contracts related to E-rate eligible and funded equipment or services, identifying the contract term (start and end dates) and signed and dated by both parties (beneficiary and service provider).	
2. Notice of Award for all (E-rate eligible and funded) Contracts.	
3. Copies of all bids received and documentation supporting the award decision.	
4. Documented bidding policies and procedures and evidence of compliance with state and local procurement/bid requirements.	
5. Request for proposals and responses relating to E-rate eligible/funded contracts.	
6. Copies of all change orders or documentation for verbal change orders.	
IV. OTHER	
1. All correspondence with SLD or service providers relating to funding (including copies of the Application and other documentation submitted as part of the funding process) and funding reimbursement.	
2. Documented policies and procedures governing the Application and E-rate funded procurement, expenditure, and reimbursement processes.	
3. Detailed listing by Funding Year, of all E-rate funded equipment and services provided by item, description of equipment or service, cost and location (see also item III. 6.).	
4. Proof of notification and refund of any amounts due back to SLD as a result of identified over-claims, errors resulting in over-payments or any other situation in which funds are required to be returned.	

Figure 4–1 *continued*

Coordination with Finance Staff

Meeting with the business office or finance director is another step in the coordination of grants management. The terms and conditions related to the finances of the project should be reviewed with the project director. If there is more than one finance department staff member, it may be helpful to assign one person to the grant. Staff should review the terms and conditions to identify allowable budget expenses and to review any restrictions related to purchases with grant funds.

Both project staff and finance staff should clarify their roles and responsibilities. For example, if the project director submits a budget revision to the funder and it is approved, this revision must be given to the finance department. Or the finance department should review grant expenditures, and if there are concerns, the department should share them with the project director.

If the funder has specific financial forms that must be used, these should be shared also. (See **Figure 4–2** and **Figure 4–3** for the short and long Financial Status Report forms required by many federal funders.) Funders may provide specific templates of time sheets (see **Figure 4–4** for the Sample Personnel Activity Report form from the National Endowment for the Arts) or expenditure reports, for example. If funders provide specific templates, these are required, and the funder will not accept reports that an organization has created and currently uses.

The project director and finance director should discuss the audit procedure and the documentation that will be needed for the audit. After an audit is completed, the finance staff should meet with the project director to review the results.

Both project and financial staff must review the tracking of matching funds throughout the project and if needed, develop a form to document this information. Some of the matching funds may be in the form of in-kind contributions and must be documented just like the cash that is contributed to the project. As an additional documentation of matching funds, the finance department may want to send an acknowledgement letter to all contributors of matching funds.

Coordination with the Evaluator

A meeting should be scheduled with the evaluator and the project director to discuss the timing of evaluation activities and the types of evaluation tools that will be used. In some cases, evaluation tools that are specific to the project will need to be developed. After this preliminary meeting is held, if the project staff will play a role in the project evaluation, they, too, should meet with the evaluator. Topics to discuss may include an explanation of the evaluation tools and the procedures that will be used for staff to collect data during the project.

Chapter Summary

One of the keys to effective grants management is planning and preparing early in the process, shortly after a grant award has been accepted. Coordination with project staff, the financial office, and the evaluator are all critical to the process. Creating grant files for each funded project is a necessity and will also make the audit process easier. Creating review schedules and responsibility charts will help to keep information organized, especially for grantees with multiple, simultaneous grants.

FINANCIAL STATUS REPORT
(Short Form)
(Follow instructions on the back)

1. Federal Agency and Organizational Element to Which Report is Submitted	2. Federal Grant or Other Identifying Number Assigned By Federal Agency	OMB Approval No. **0348-0038**	Page of pages

3. Recipient Organization (Name and complete address, including ZIP code)

4. Employer Identification Number	5. Recipient Account Number or Identifying Number	6. Final Report ☐ Yes ☐ No	7. Basis ☐ Cash ☐ Accrual

8. Funding/Grant Period *(See instructions)* From: (Month, Day, Year)	To: (Month, Day, Year)	9. Period Covered by this Report From: (Month, Day, Year)	To: (Month, Day, Year)

10. Transactions:	I Previously Reported	II This Period	III Cumulative
a. Total outlays			0.00
b. Recipient share of outlays			0.00
c. Federal share of outlays	0.00	0.00	0.00
d. Total unliquidated obligations			
e. Recipient share of unliquidated obligations			
f. Federal share of unliquidated obligations			
g. Total Federal share (Sum of lines c and f)			0.00
h. Total Federal funds authorized for this funding period			
i. Unobligated balance of Federal funds (Line h minus line g)			0.00

11. Indirect Expense	a. Type of Rate (Place "X" in appropriate box) ☐ Provisional ☐ Predetermined ☐ Final ☐ Fixed			
	b. Rate	c. Base	d. Total Amount	e. Federal Share

12. Remarks: Attach any explanations deemed necessary or information required by Federal sponsoring agency in compliance with governing legislation.

13. Certification: I certify to the best of my knowledge and belief that this report is correct and complete and that all outlays and unliquidated obligations are for the purposes set forth in the award documents.

Typed or Printed Name and Title	Telephone (Area code, number and extension)
Signature of Authorized Certifying Official	Date Report Submitted

NSN 7540-01-218-4387   269-202   Standard Form 269A (Rev. 7-97)
Prescribed by OMB Circulars A-102 and A-110

(continues)

Figure 4–2 *Short Financial Status form (Form 269A).*
Source: *Office of Management and Budget, United States Government.*

FINANCIAL STATUS REPORT
(Short Form)

Public reporting burden for this collection of information is estimated to average 90 minutes per response, including time for reviewing instructions, searching existing data sources, gathering and maintaining the data needed, and completing and reviewing the collection of information. Send comments regarding the burden estimate or any other aspect of this collection of information, including suggestions for reducing this burden, to the Office of Management and Budget, Paperwork Reduction Project (0348-0038), Washington, DC 20503.

PLEASE DO NOT RETURN YOUR COMPLETED FORM TO THE OFFICE OF MANAGEMENT AND BUDGET. SEND IT TO THE ADDRESS PROVIDED BY THE SPONSORING AGENCY.

Please type or print legibly. The following general instructions explain how to use the form itself. You may need additional information to complete certain items correctly, or to decide whether a specific item is applicable to this award. Usually, such information will be found in the Federal agency's grant regulations or in the terms and conditions of the award. You may also contact the Federal agency directly.

Item	Entry

1, 2 and 3. Self-explanatory.

4. Enter the Employer Identification Number (EIN) assigned by the U.S. Internal Revenue Service.

5. Space reserved for an account number or other identifying number assigned by the recipient.

6. Check *yes* only if this is the last report for the period shown in item 8.

7. Self-explanatory.

8. Unless you have received other instructions from the awarding agency, enter the beginning and ending dates of the current funding period. If this is a multi-year program, the Federal agency might require cumulative reporting through consecutive funding periods. In that case, enter the beginning and ending dates of the grant period, and in the rest of these instructions, substitute the term "grant period" for "funding period."

9. Self-explanatory.

10. The purpose of columns I, II, and III is to show the effect of this reporting period's transactions on cumulative financial status. The amounts entered in column I will normally be the same as those in column III of the previous report in *the same funding period*. If this is the first or only report of the funding period, leave columns I and II blank. If you need to adjust amounts entered on previous reports, footnote the column I entry on this report and attach an explanation.

10a. Enter total program outlays less any rebates, refunds, or other credits. For reports prepared on a cash basis, outlays are the sum of actual cash disbursements for direct costs for goods and services, the amount of indirect expense charged, the value of in-kind contributions applied, and the amount of cash advances and payments made to subrecipients. For reports prepared on an accrual basis, outlays are the sum of actual cash disbursements for direct charges for goods and services, the amount of indirect expense incurred,

the value of in-kind contributions applied, and the net increase or decrease in the amounts owed by the recipient for goods and other property received, for services performed by employees, contractors, subgrantees and other payees, and other amounts becoming owed under programs for which no current services or performances are required, such as annuities, insurance claims, and other benefit payments.

10b. Self-explanatory.

10c. Self-explanatory.

10d. Enter the total amount of unliquidated obligations, including unliquidated obligations to subgrantees and contractors.

Unliquidated obligations on a cash basis are obligations incurred, but not yet paid. On an accrual basis, they are obligations incurred, but for which an outlay has not yet been recorded.

Do not include any amounts on line 10d that have been included on lines 10a, b, or c.

On the final report, line 10d must be zero.

10e. f, g, h, h and i. Self-explanatory.

11a. Self-explanatory.

11b. Enter the indirect cost rate in effect during the reporting period.

11c. Enter the amount of the base against which the rate was applied.

11d. Enter the total amount of indirect costs charged during the report period.

11e. Enter the Federal share of the amount in 11d.

Note: If more than one rate was in effect during the period shown in item 8, attach a schedule showing the bases against which the different rates were applied, the respective rates, the calendar periods they were in effect, amounts of indirect expense charged to the project, and the Federal share of indirect expense charged to the project to date.

SF-269A (Rev. 7-97) Back

Figure 4–2 *continued*

FINANCIAL STATUS REPORT
(Long Form)
(Follow instructions on the back)

1. Federal Agency and Organizational Element to Which Report is Submitted	2. Federal Grant or Other Identifying Number Assigned By Federal Agency	OMB Approval No. **0348-0039**	Page of pages

3. Recipient Organization (Name and complete address, including ZIP code)

4. Employer Identification Number	5. Recipient Account Number or Identifying Number	6. Final Report ☐ Yes ☐ No	7. Basis ☐ Cash ☐ Accrual

8. Funding/Grant Period *(See instructions)* From: (Month, Day, Year) — To: (Month, Day, Year)	9. Period Covered by this Report From: (Month, Day, Year) — To: (Month, Day, Year)

10. Transactions:	I Previously Reported	II This Period	III Cumulative
a. Total outlays			0.00
b. Refunds, rebates, etc.			0.00
c. Program income used in accordance with the deduction alternative			0.00
d. Net outlays *(Line a, less the sum of lines b and c)*	0.00	0.00	0.00
Recipient's share of net outlays, consisting of:			
e. Third party (in-kind) contributions			0.00
f. Other Federal awards authorized to be used to match this award			0.00
g. Program income used in accordance with the matching or cost sharing alternative			0.00
h. All other recipient outlays not shown on lines e, f or g			0.00
i. Total recipient share of net outlays *(Sum of lines e, f, g and h)*	0.00	0.00	0.00
j. Federal share of net outlays *(line d less line i)*	0.00	0.00	0.00
k. Total unliquidated obligations			
l. Recipient's share of unliquidated obligations			
m. Federal share of unliquidated obligations			
n. Total Federal share *(sum of lines j and m)*			0.00
o. Total Federal funds authorized for this funding period			
p. Unobligated balance of Federal funds *(Line o minus line n)*			0.00
Program income, consisting of:			
q. Disbursed program income shown on lines c and/or g above			
r. Disbursed program income using the addition alternative			
s. Undisbursed program income			
t. Total program income realized *(Sum of lines q, r and s)*			0.00

11. Indirect Expense	a. Type of Rate *(Place "X" in appropriate box)* ☐ Provisional ☐ Predetermined ☐ Final ☐ Fixed			
	b. Rate	c. Base	d. Total Amount	e. Federal Share

12. Remarks: Attach any explanations deemed necessary or information required by Federal sponsoring agency in compliance with governing legislation.

13. Certification: **I certify to the best of my knowledge and belief that this report is correct and complete and that all outlays and unliquidated obligations are for the purposes set forth in the award documents.**

Typed or Printed Name and Title	Telephone (Area code, number and extension)
Signature of Authorized Certifying Official	Date Report Submitted June 16, 2009

Previous Edition Usable
NSN 7540-01-012-4285

269-104

200-498 P.O. 139 (Face)

Standard Form 269 (Rev. 7-97)
Prescribed by OMB Circulars A-102 and A-110

(continues)

Figure 4–3 *Long Financial Status form (Form 269).*
Source: *Office of Management and Budget, United States Government.*

FINANCIAL STATUS REPORT
(Long Form)

Public reporting burden for this collection of information is estimated to average 30 minutes per response, including time for reviewing instructions, searching existing data sources, gathering and maintaining the data needed, and completing and reviewing the collection of information. Send comments regarding the burden estimate or any other aspect of this collection of information, including suggestions for reducing this burden, to the Office of Management and Budget, Paperwork Reduction Project (0348-0039), Washington, DC 20503.

PLEASE <u>DO NOT</u> RETURN YOUR COMPLETED FORM TO THE OFFICE OF MANAGEMENT AND BUDGET.

Please type or print legibly. The following general instructions explain how to use the form itself. You may need additional information to complete certain items correctly, or to decide whether a specific item is applicable to this award. Usually, such information will be found in the Federal agency's grant regulations or in the terms and conditions of the award (e.g., how to calculate the Federal share, the permissible uses of program income, the value of in-kind contributions, etc.). You may also contact the Federal agency directly.

Item	Entry	Item	Entry

1, 2 and 3. Self-explanatory.

4. Enter the Employer Identification Number (EIN) assigned by the U.S. Internal Revenue Service.

5. Space reserved for an account number or other identifying number assigned by the recipient.

6. Check *yes* only if this is the last report for the period shown in item 8.

7. Self-explanatory.

8. Unless you have received other instructions from the awarding agency, enter the beginning and ending dates of the current funding period. If this is a multi-year program, the Federal agency might require cumulative reporting through consecutive funding periods. In that case, enter the beginning and ending dates of the grant period, and in the rest of these instructions, substitute the term "grant period" for "funding period."

9. Self-explanatory.

10. The purpose of columns, I, II, and III is to show the effect of this reporting period's transactions on cumulative financial status. The amounts entered in column I will normally be the same as those in column III of the previous report *in the same funding period*. If this is the first or only report of the funding period, leave columns I and II blank. If you need to adjust amounts entered on previous reports, footnote the column I entry on this report and attach an explanation.

10a. Enter total gross program outlays. Include disbursements of cash realized as program income if that income will also be shown on lines 10c or 10g. Do not include program income that will be shown on lines 10r or 10s.

For reports prepared on a cash basis, outlays are the sum of actual cash disbursements for direct costs for goods and services, the amount of indirect expense charged, the value of in-kind contributions applied, and the amount of cash advances and payments made to subrecipients. For reports prepared on an accrual basis, outlays are the sum of actual cash disbursements for direct charges for goods and services, the amount of indirect expense incurred, the value of in-kind contributions applied, and the net increase or decrease in the amounts owed by the recipient for goods and other property received, for services performed by employees, contractors, subgrantees and other payees, and other amounts becoming owed under programs for which no current services or performances are required, such as annuities, insurance claims, and other benefit payments.

10b. Enter any receipts related to outlays reported on the form that are being treated as a reduction of expenditure rather than income, and were not already netted out of the amount shown as outlays on line 10a.

10c. Enter the amount of program income that was used in accordance with the deduction alternative.

Note: Program income used in accordance with other alternatives is entered on lines q, r, and s. Recipients reporting on a cash basis should enter the amount of cash income received; on an accrual basis, enter the program income earned. Program income may or may not have been included in an application budget and/or a budget on the award document. If actual income is from a different source or is significantly different in amount, attach an explanation or use the remarks section.

10d, e, f, g, h, i and j. Self-explanatory.

10k. Enter the total amount of unliquidated obligations, including unliquidated obligations to subgrantees and contractors.

Unliquidated obligations on a cash basis are obligations incurred, but not yet paid. On an accrual basis, they are obligations incurred, but for which an outlay has not been recorded.

Do not include any amounts on line 10k that have been included on lines 10a and 10j.

On the final report, line 10k must be zero.

10l. Self-explanatory.

10m. On the final report, line 10m must also be zero.

10n, o, p, q, r, s and t. Self-explanatory.

11a. Self-explanatory.

11b. Enter the indirect cost rate in effect during the reporting period.

11c. Enter the amount of the base against which the rate was applied.

11d. Enter the total amount of indirect costs charged during the report period.

11e. Enter the Federal share of the amount in 11d.

Note: If more than one rate was in effect during the period shown in item 8, attach a schedule showing the bases against which the different rates were applied, the respective rates, the calendar periods they were in effect, amounts of indirect expense charged to the project, and the Federal share of indirect expense charged to the project to date.

SF-269 Back (Rev. 7-97)

Figure 4–3 *continued*

**SAMPLE PERSONNEL ACTIVITY REPORT
(TIME AND EFFORT REPORT)**

Organization Name:_____

Employee's Name_____   Week Ending _____

Activity	Distribution of Time
Arts Endowment	
1. Grant..	_____ %
2. Grant..	_____ %
Other	
3. Project name...	_____ %
4. Project name...	_____ %
5. Project name...	_____ %
Administrative..	_____ %
Fundraising...	_____ %
Leave	
Sick...	_____ %
Vacation/annual...	_____ %
Other (specify)	_____ %
TOTAL:	_100_ %

Employee's Signature _____   Date:_____

Supervisor's Signature _____   Date:_____

In preparing personnel activity reports, please note the following:

- The reports must be based on an after-the-fact determination of the employee's actual activities (i.e., these cannot be estimated in advance). For example, the distribution of time might be determined based on notes from personal calendars and/or reasonable estimates of time spent on various activities.

- All of the employee's compensated time must be accounted for in these reports. This would include time spent on activities in addition to the Endowment-supported project(s), as well as leave (sick/vacation/holiday), administrative duties, etc. NOTE: **For nonprofessional employees, grantees must also maintain records indicating the total number of hours worked each day in conformance with the Fair Labor Standards Act (29 CFR Part 516).**

- The reports must be signed by the employee or a responsible supervisory official.

- Reports must coincide with one or more pay periods and be used to reconcile salary and fringe benefit costs to appropriate accounts on a regular (preferably monthly) basis.

- Unless otherwise specified in the grant award letter or if the organizations is on either working capital advance or cost reimbursement method of funding, the Endowment waives the requirement to maintain personnel activity reports for nonprofit organizations and institutions of higher education receiving an award of less than $50,000 starting with year 2005 awards. However, appropriate records must be maintained to verify any expenses attributed to Federal/matching funds.

Figure 4–4 *Sample Personnel Activity Report form.*
Source: National Endowment for the Arts.

Chapter 5

Evaluation

The evaluation section of a grant proposal is more than likely one of the most important sections. Funders want to make sure that their dollars are being wisely invested in a project that has an impact, and they want to be sure that grantees have the tools to measure their objectives. Carrying out the evaluation process is an important piece of managing a grant, and the evaluation should be done throughout the implementation of the project.

History of Evaluation Research

What is the purpose of evaluation? According to author W. Lawrence Neuman in his book *Social Research Methods*, evaluation research is conducted to learn "whether a program or activity accomplished its intended objectives" (2005, p. 524). Neuman goes on to state that evaluation can be qualitative or quantitative. The most common audience for evaluation is "stakeholders or parties with a stake in a project such as program staff, beneficiaries of services, or collaborative organizations" (p. 524).

It is interesting to note that Neuman (2005) traces the growth of evaluation research directly to the growth of government social programs. He states that the primary reason for that growth was political, saying that criticisms of the social programs began during the 1960s. The critics demanded empirical data that proved that the programs were meeting their objectives and were not a waste of taxpayers' money.

According to Neuman (2005), a second reason for the growth of evaluation research was the desire to compare and measure the effectiveness of alternative programs or methods of delivering services. Even today, the reasons Neuman attributes to the growth of evaluation continue to support the inclusion of evaluation sections in proposals, and the process of evaluating grant-funded projects.

Types of Evaluation

For grantees, the two most common forms of evaluation are the formative evaluation and the summative evaluation.

A formative evaluation is conducted throughout a project. The advantage of conducting a formative evaluation is that if objectives are not being met, grantees can make needed corrections to ensure the success of the project.

On the other hand, a summative evaluation is conducted at the end of the project, and results are reported. If any objectives were not met, the grantee, with the evaluator's assistance, can only report what the cause might be.

Due to the costs incurred, most funders only require a summative evaluation. However, grantees who conduct both formative and summative types can strengthen their project by constantly monitoring its success. Before placing both types in the proposal, grantees should read the request for proposal carefully to see what type of evaluation is required, they should look at allowable budget items to see if an external evaluator can be hired, and they should decide if an external evaluation will be too costly if it is not an allowable item.

Choosing an Evaluator

When grantees use internal evaluators, they often select a staff member who has experience with data collection and interpretation. Choosing an external evaluator can be difficult if the grantee has no prior experience with one. In addition, grantees must compare the costs of external evaluators and determine which individual is the best choice—keeping available grant funding in mind.

Grantees may find it helpful to contact prior grantees and ask who performed their external evaluation. By selecting one of these evaluators, the grantee knows that the evaluator has experience with the grant program. Sometimes the funder may be able to provide a list of potential evaluators or may have a preference for who the grantee uses to evaluate the project.

Using a Logic Model

A logic model is a common evaluation tool used by grantees. It is used to develop an outcome-based evaluation process that systematically assesses the extent to which a project meets its intended goals. Rather than measuring success by merely looking at the reasonableness of the budget, the low percentage of administrative costs, or the volume of services provided, the logic model focuses on the beneficial results of a project and assesses both the short- and long-term impacts.

The components of a logic model include:

1. The *inputs* or resources that the grantee will need to allocate in order for a project to be successful. Some examples include staff, volunteers, facilities, equipment, and materials.

2. The *activities* or services that will occur in order to attain goals and objectives. Some examples include training, providing information or services, counseling, and developing programs.

3. The *outputs* or numbers that indicate the successful attainment of the activities, usually expressed in the number of participants in the project, the products generated, and the quantity of services that were provided. Some examples include 25 training sessions to 75 attendees and 350 referrals to the counseling program.

4. The *outcomes/impacts* or benefits that describe the changes produced as a consequence of participating in the project; changes in participants' level of knowledge, skills, or behaviors; or changes in the community as a result of the project. Some examples include a reduction in the number of homeless individuals, a decrease in the community unemployment rate, and the number of project participants remaining drug free 1 year after being in the project.

After the Evaluation Is Conducted

Many funders will require the submission of an evaluation report when the project period comes to an end. In fact, some funders may connect the receipt of the final award payment to the receipt of an evaluation report.

After gathering data related to each objective, an evaluator should judge how well each objective was met and communicate this in the final report. Neuman (2005) cautions that individuals can "use, ignore, or misuse the results of evaluation research" (p. 528). To prevent this, he suggests that in the final report, evaluators include concrete recommendations with timelines and multiple methods of collecting data.

Some funders will ask how a grantee plans to disseminate the information from the project. Neuman recommends that the evaluation results of a project be widely distributed. Grantees might want to consider distributing the report to a variety of stakeholders, local media, and legislators and putting the report on their Web site. Neuman suggests a variety of formats be used to distribute the results, including a short version or executive summary, a long version (the entire report), and a series of oral presentations to a variety of audiences including professional colleagues (2005).

Conversation with an Evaluator

The following information regarding evaluations was provided by Dr. Matt Rearick (personal communication, 2008), an evaluator who is currently an assistant professor of health, education, and human performance at Roanoke College in Virginia. Dr. Rearick has experience conducting external evaluations for several grant-funded projects.

What are three to five of the most common types of evaluation tools included in proposals?

1. *Logic models*—Logic models are general frameworks that answer the following four questions about a project: (1) What are the inputs (people, places, things)? (2) What are the activities (programs, resources, and equipment)? (3) What are the outputs (what the grantee expects to see based on the inputs and activities)? and (4) What are the outcomes (what the grantee expects to see as a result of achieving the project's goals)?

   Logic models are visual and often look like a flowchart and so are often easier to understand than a narrative description in a proposal. A proposal does not need to include a logic model to have structure or a disciplined assessment and evaluation, but their inherent clarity and the discipline that goes into creating one help everyone—proposal reviewers, proposal writers, stakeholders, and evaluators—comprehend the project's logic and flow. Logic models are often the first step in determining what types of evaluation tools are necessary for a project.

2. *Quasi-experimental evaluation designs*—Experimental designs (i.e., experimental vs. control groups) are preferred in research. Yet, in most grant programs, this is difficult to implement for the following three reasons: (1) limited funds; (2) buy-in/adherence; and (3) desire on the part of the grantee to include all participants in the project, rather than excluding some individuals. As an alternative, quasi-experimental designs can be used. A grantee can use comparison groups or use participants as their own control group by pretesting and posttesting them.

   There are inherent problems, however, using quasi-experimental designs when trying to ascertain causality. The advantage of the effectiveness for evaluating a grant program, combined with the potential for lowering costs and lessening the full burden of experimental designs, makes this type of design appealing to funders who are often attracted to research-oriented approaches.

3. *Well-established tools such as surveys, questionnaires, and examinations*— Grantees should use well-respected and research-established surveys and exams whenever possible. These have been tested for reliability and valid-

ity and give evaluators, project staff, and funders the greatest degree of confidence when examining data for trends and significant findings.

4. *Project-specific surveys, questionnaires, and examinations*—Every grant-funded project is unique, and using already-established tools described in No. 3 may not capture all that is happening in every project. Developing tools unique to the specific project that ask specific questions related to it is good and complementary to any well-established tools. To increase the scope of the assessment and evaluation, grantees should consider using both well-established tools and those that have been developed specifically for the project.

5. *Interviews*—Part of the evaluation process can and, in many cases, should include interviews with project staff, participants, and other stakeholders. Interviews can be structured or unstructured. Like No. 3 and No. 4, interviews should not be the sole evaluation tool, but they should be seen as complementary to other assessment tools being utilized.

What elements make up a successful collaboration between an evaluator and project staff?

1. *A priori communication*—Whenever possible, the evaluator should be involved at the onset of project conception and development. Many grantees will wait until after they receive notice of a grant award to find and hire an evaluator, which can lead to several problems. When an evaluator is hired in the early stages before the proposal is even submitted, he/she can arrange the project design so that data are collected easily and can make sure that answers to questions are based on using reliable techniques. Evaluators can also help with the development of the project's logic model and assist with making sure it is well articulated in the proposal.

2. *Explanation of how the data will be collected and used*—Most, if not all, project staff want to continuously improve their project; however, in order to do this, staff need to understand how and why the information that an evaluator collects will help them make these improvements. Without this understanding at the beginning of the project, data collection will feel like one more activity staff has to carry out, and it may seem burdensome. Evaluators should function as teachers or facilitators, and staff should be willing to understand data collection and interpretation in a new way. These discussions between the evaluator and the project staff should take place before implementation so everyone is clear about what the expectations are and what is possible.

3. *Understanding that evaluations serve several groups*—Grantees sometimes make the mistake of thinking that the sole job of the evaluator is to report findings to the funder. This is actually only half of the evaluator's job. The

other is to help project staff use information (data collected) in a new way and to look at their project in a more comprehensive light. The information that an evaluator collects is complementary to what the project staff know or are also collecting about their project. Grantees and project staff should understand that during the project implementation phase that they have an expert in project assessment at their disposal. They need to maximize the presence of the evaluator so that when funding ends from the grantor, they have gained new tools and strategies for tracking their own program development and performance. In some respects, this is a form of sustainability after the funding period ends.

Chapter Summary

Evaluation is a critical component of both the grant proposal and the grants management process. Grantees are usually expected to carry out a summative evaluation; however, conducting a formative evaluation can strengthen the proposal and make the project even more successful.

Hiring an external evaluator can be costly; however, grantors who expect one to be involved in the project will include these costs as allowable budget items. Grants managers should work with an evaluator from the beginning of the project design so he or she has an idea of the scope of the evaluation that needs to be completed and can make suggestions for evaluation tools. Tools specific to the project may have to be developed. Ongoing communication between staff and an evaluator is encouraged.

Reference

Neuman, W. L. (2005). *Social research methods*, Allyn and Bacon, Needham Heights, MA.

Chapter 6

Audits and Monitoring Visits

The purpose of an audit is to form a view as to whether the information presented in financial reports on a specific date actually reflect the financial position of an organization. As a part of the application process, funders may ask for the most recent copy of the applicant's audit. Typically, this request is made by private funders rather than public funders, and they often are hesitant to award funds if there is no audit report. Public funders may ask for a single audit of grant funds after a project is completed if a grantee expends a specific amount of federal funds during a project period of 12 months.

Office of Management and Budget Circulars

The federal Office of Management and Budget (OMB) develops government-wide policies to make sure that federal grants are managed properly and that all federal funds are spent according to laws and regulations that are applicable to specific grant programs. These circulars are especially important when managing federal grants.

On the OMB Web site, www.whitehouse.gov/omb/circulars/, 30 circulars are listed. The majority of grantees should familiarize themselves with A-21, A-110, and A-133; however, other circulars may be applicable to specific grants and should be read also.

OMB Circular A-21 (1998) is titled *Cost Principles for Educational Institutions*. This circular establishes principles for determining costs applicable to grants, contracts, and other agreements with educational institutions. According to this document:

> all Federal agencies that sponsor research and development, training and other work at educational institutions shall apply the provisions of this Circular in determining the costs incurred for such work. The principles shall also be used as a guide in the pricing of fixed price or lump sum agreements. (p. 2, Section 3, Applicability)

OMB Circular A-110 is called the *Grants and Cooperative Agreements for Grants and Other Agreements with institutions of Higher Education, Hospitals and Other Non-Profit Organizations*. This circular sets standards for obtaining consistency and uniformity among federal agencies in the administration of grants to and agreements with grantees including institutions of higher education, hospitals, and other non-profit organizations. The principles in the circular explain how the grantees must do business with the grantor, the financial systems that the grantee must put into place, and how the grantees must administer the awards. This circular does not apply to state and local governments acting as grantees; a separate circular, A-102, sets the standards for them.

OMB Circular A-133, *Audits of States, Local Governments and Non-Profit Organizations*, sets the standards for consistency and uniformity among federal agents for the audit of grantees including state and local governments and nonprofit organizations that receive federal funds. The circular includes information about audit requirements, program-specific audits, auditee responsibilities, selecting an auditor, and follow-up to audit findings.

The Importance of an Audit

Conducting an annual audit that examines revenue and expenditures is a sound business practice. It illustrates that an organization is using funds in an appropriate manner. Audits can also identify problems with how a grantee has spent grant funds or if a grantee has complied with the terms and conditions of a grant. The terms and conditions are found in the paperwork an applicant receives when an award is offered.

Types of Audits

A single audit is required if an organization expends more than $500,000 in federal funds in 1 year. The single audit is an organization-wide audit that will include an examination of all grant funds. Auditors will check to see if grant fund transactions are properly documented and recorded according to generally accepted accounting principles.

If a federal grant program's rules and regulations do not require a single audit, a grantee may request a program-specific audit. In this case, an auditor will only examine the grant funds of a specific grant program, checking that the transaction documentation and recording are done according to generally accepted accounting principles.

Preparing for an Audit

Grantees should have the following information ready for an auditor to review:

- A list of all funders, the program officer name for federal grants, the foundation officer name for private funding, and address
- The dates of a grant period for each grant awarded
- The dollar amount of each grant awarded
- The date that any grant was received
- Any restrictions associated with the grant (this information should be included in the program guidance)
- Copies of every submitted, funded proposal
- Copies of every award notification communication

Figure 4–1 is a sample list for recipients of the Universal Services Administrative Fund who are going to be audited by the Universal Service Administrative Company and the Federal Communications Commission.

Contents of an Audit Report

After an auditor is finished with the audit, an audit report is provided to the organization. Typically, this report will include:

- An opinion letter
- Financial statements with explanations found in footnotes
- A compliance statement
- If applicable, an opinion letter that addresses compliance with grants terms and conditions

The opinion letter makes a comment about the financial statements the auditor includes in the audit report. The opinion is effective on the specific date that the statements were reviewed. The financial statements include a balance sheet, an income statement, a cash flow statement, and notes summarizing significant accounting policies. Auditors may also include an overall opinion based on the severity of the audit issues in the report. Auditors might include an opinion relating specifically to grant funds and the terms and conditions of the grant program.

Auditors sometimes issue audit findings. These are areas of weakness, policy violation, financial misstatements, or other issues that are identified during the audit process. Material findings must be taken very seriously by grantees, especially if they involve grant funds. Some examples of material findings include questionable costs, failing to meet specific grant terms and/or conditions, buying unallowable items with grant funds, or failing to meet a matching fund requirement.

Material findings must be reported to the funder of the grant program involved. If an audit of a grantee of federal funds includes any material findings, grantees are responsible for follow-up and corrective action. Grantees will be asked to develop a corrective action plan that must be submitted to the funder for approval. In subsequent years of a multiyear grant, grantees must file a summary schedule of prior audit findings and the status of the corrective action.

Failure to respond to material findings can result in significant financial and programmatic penalties for a grantee. This, in turn, can have long-term implications as other federal agencies and/or private funders may not be willing to offer a grant award to a grantee who has ignored material findings during an audit.

Monitoring Visits

During the implementation of a project, funders may conduct a monitoring visit. The best way to determine the reason for a monitoring visit is to ask the funder directly. Grantees should not always assume that these visits are cause for alarm because there is a problem or a concern. The purpose of this type of visit is often to review documents, data collection procedures, and fiscal documents to make sure that everything is being done correctly. If a monitoring review is scheduled, the grant manager should ask the funder about the specific documents that should be ready for examination.

Finding out what the funder wants to accomplish during the visit will assist the grantee with planning and preparing for the visit. It is wise to create an agenda for the visit with input from the funder. Be clear about the purpose of the visit and the funder's objective(s) for the visit. Find out if a funder wants to meet with project staff and/or participants.

If the purpose of the monitoring visit is to address a problem or concern, be sure to work with the funder to resolve it. Provide reasonable explanations if requested, and be open to suggestions about how to make any improvements to the project or to the management of the grant.

Chapter Summary

Audits are an important part of the grants management process, and an audit of grant funds may be required by funders. Grants managers should work with the auditor and be prepared with all documents to be examined. If the audit report is unfavorable, the grant manager should prepare a course of corrective action and work diligently on the material findings. Grantees should also be familiar with the OMB circulars that impact their federal grants.

Monitoring visits are a normal part of the grants management process and should not cause alarm. Grantees should be fully prepared for the visit, with all documents ready for review.

Reference

Office of Management and Budget. (1998). *Cost principles for educational institutions* (OMB Circular A-21). Available from www.whitehouse.gov/omb/circulars/.

Chapter 7

Grants Management of Federal Grants

As the samples included in this chapter will show, applicants who accept awards from public funders, especially federal agencies, have substantial paperwork to complete as a part of the management of the grant. This paperwork can include information from the Office of Management and Budget (OMB) circulars, specific grant policy manuals that can be downloaded from the Internet, and a variety of grant report templates to complete and submit.

Office of Management and Budget Circulars

The Office of Management and Budget develops government-wide policies to ensure that grants are managed properly and that the federal grant dollars received by grantees are spent according to applicable regulations and laws.

On its Web site, www.whitehouse.gov/omb/, there are more than 25 circulars listed. Fortunately, the majority of grantees only need to read and be familiar with the following three:

1. OMB Circular A-21
2. OMB Circular A-110
3. OMB Circular A-133

These three circulars deal primarily with funds and audits and were discussed in Chapter 6.

Grant Performance Reports

If the grantor does not include grants management information in the original request for proposal, it will be included in the paperwork that accompanies the acceptance document. Many public funders now post the information on their Web sites.

Grantors have different requirements for the information that should be included in grant performance reports. **Figure 7–1** is the instructions for reports for grants issued by the U.S. Department of Education, **Figure 7–2** for reports for the National Endowment for the Humanities, and **Figure 7–3** for reports for the Institute of Museum and Library Services.

Generally, these samples show that grantees must document and report their progress towards meeting the objectives that were stated in their approved grant proposal. The U.S. Department of Education asks grantees to establish performance measures for each objective and use the project status chart (see Figure 7–1c) to document their status.

The National Endowment for the Humanities (NEH) does not have a specific form to complete; however, the agency does ask grantees to provide similar information in a narrative format. The NEH grant performance reporting requirements ask for more information than just responding to performance measures and objectives. This document (see Figure 7–2) supports the need for project staff to be aware at the beginning of the project of the types of data that will need to be collected during project implementation.

Many of these reporting requirements ask grantees to report on what can be termed *negative results*. For example, the Institute of Museum and Library Services requirements (see Figure 7–3) ask grantees to provide an explanation if the project schedule has not been met and the steps that the grantee will take to correct this. The U.S. Department of Education asks for similar explanations (see No. 3 under Explanation of Progress, in Figure 7–1).

All project staff and the project evaluator should receive copies of the reporting requirements in the early weeks of the project. Based on the reporting requirements, specific data collection forms can be developed, or the sample forms provided by the funder can be completed during the project rather than waiting until midyear or the end of the project and trying to find data that, in fact, may not have been collected.

Importance of Calendars

Grantees, especially those who are managing several federal grants simultaneously, must have a calendar. Because the funding time frames can be very similar for

INSTRUCTIONS FOR GRANT PERFORMANCE REPORT (ED 524B)

PURPOSE

Recipients of multi-year discretionary grants must submit an annual performance report for each year funding has been approved in order to receive a continuation award. The annual performance report should demonstrate whether substantial progress has been made toward meeting the project objectives and the program performance measures. The information described in these instructions will provide the U.S. Department of Education (ED) with the information needed to determine whether recipients have demonstrated substantial progress. ED program offices may also require recipients of "forward funded" grants that are awarded funds for their entire multi-year project up-front in a single grant award to submit the Grant Performance Report (ED 524B) on an annual basis. In addition, ED program offices may also require recipients to use the ED 524B to submit their final performance reports. Performance reporting requirements are found in 34 CFR 74.51, 75.118, 75.253, 75.590 and 80.40 of the Education Department General Administrative Regulations (EDGAR).

GENERAL INSTRUCTIONS

- Please read the attached "Dear Colleague Letter" from your program office carefully. It contains specific instructions for completing the ED 524B for your program.

- You must submit the ED 524B Cover Sheet, Executive Summary, and Project Status Chart. You may reference sections and page numbers of your approved application rather than repeating information.

- Please follow the appropriate instructions depending on whether you are submitting an annual performance report or a final performance report.

- If you are submitting a paper copy of the ED 524B, please submit one original and one copy. ED program offices will notify grant recipients of the due date for submission of annual performance reports; however, general guidelines are provided below in the instructions for ED 524B Cover Sheet, item 7. Reporting Period. Final performance reports are due 90 days after the expiration of the grant's project period (performance period).

  Note: For the purposes of this report, the term "project period" is used interchangeably with the term "performance period," which is found on the Grant Award Notification (GAN).

- Many programs provide grantees with the option of completing and submitting the ED 524B online through e-Reports. Please follow instructions from your program office regarding the use of e-Reports for submitting your ED 524B.

- For those programs that operate under statutes or regulations that require additional or different reporting for performance or monitoring purposes, ED program offices will inform you when this additional or different reporting should be made.

INSTRUCTIONS FOR THE ED 524B COVER SHEET

Complete the ED 524B Cover Sheet with the appropriate information. Instructions for items 1, 3, 4 and 6 are included on the ED 524B Cover Sheet. Instructions for items 2 and 5 and items 7 through 12 are included in this instruction sheet.

2. **Grantee NCES ID Number**

   -- **Annual and Final Performance Reports:**

(continues)

Figure 7–1a *Instructions for grant reports.*
Source: *United States Department of Education.*

Please enter the current National Center for Education Statistics (NCES) ID number of the grantee. Grantees that are State Educational Agencies (SEA) should enter their state's FIPS (Federal Information Processing Standards) code in item 2. Item 2 only applies to grantees that are Institutions of Higher Education (IHE), SEAs, Local Educational Agencies (LEA), public libraries, and public, charter, and private elementary or secondary schools. Leave blank, if this item is not applicable.

Please go to the applicable website listed below to obtain the grantee's NCES ID number or FIPS code. Depending on your organization type, this number will range from 2 to 12 numeric digits.

- IHEs (IPEDS ID); Public Libraries (Library ID); and Public, Charter and Private Schools (NCES School ID): http://nces.ed.gov/globallocator
- LEAs (NCES District ID): http://nces.ed.gov/ccd/districtsearch/
- SEAs (FIPS code): To obtain your state's FIPS code, please search on any public school district in your state at: http://nces.ed.gov/ccd/districtsearch/. **The FIPS code is the first two digits of the NCES District ID number for any public school district in a state.**

Note: Newly established organizations that do not have an NCES ID number yet should leave item 2 blank. However, once the organization's NCES ID number has been established, it must be entered on all future submissions of the ED 524B.

5. Grantee Address

Instructions for Submitting Address Changes

-- Annual and Final Performance Reports:

If the address that is listed in Block 1 of your GAN has changed and you are submitting a paper copy of the ED 524B, either submit the new address in Section C (Additional Information) of the Project Status Chart or submit the change through e-Administration (annual performance reports only), the administrative action function of e-Grants.

If you are submitting the ED 524B electronically through e-Reports, you may update your address in e-Reports.

7. Reporting Period

-- Annual Performance Reports:

Due Date: Annual performance reports are typically due seven to ten months after the start of the grant's current budget period. Please follow instructions from your program office regarding the specific due date of the annual performance report for your grant.

The reporting period for the annual performance report is from the start of the current budget period through 30 days before the due date of the report. The start date for your current budget period may be found in Block 6 of the GAN. Please note, however, that complete data on performance measures for the current budget period must be submitted to ED, either with this report or as soon as they are available, but no later than the final due date specified by your ED program office. Please see instructions for items 11a. and 11b. of the ED 524B Cover Sheet and Section A (Project Objectives Information and Related Performance Measures Data) of the Project Status Chart for specific reporting requirements for performance measures data.

-- Final Performance Reports:

Due Date: Final performance reports are due 90 days after the expiration of the grant's project period. If you receive a no-cost time extension from ED for this grant, the final performance report is due 90 days after the revised project period end date. Program offices may also request an annual performance report that covers the original final budget period from grantees that receive no-cost time extensions.

Figure 7—1a *continued*

Please enter the start and end date for the final budget period of your grant from Block 6 of the GAN. The reporting period for your final performance report covers the entire final budget period of the project, except for the information in the Executive Summary and Section C (Additional Information) of the Project Status Chart, which covers the entire project period (performance period) of the project.

8. **Budget Expenditures [Also See Section B (Budget Information) of the Project Status Chart]**

   The budget expenditure information requested in items 8a. – 8c. must be completed by your Business Office.

   Note: For the purposes of this report, the term budget expenditures means allowable grant obligations incurred during the periods specified below. (See EDGAR, 34 CFR 74.2; 75.703; 75.707; and 80.3, as applicable.)

   For budget expenditures made with Federal grant funds, you must provide an explanation in Section B (Budget Information) of the Project Status Chart, if you have not drawn down funds from the Grant Administration and Payment System (GAPS) to pay for these budget expenditures.

   --Annual Performance Reports:

   - Report your actual budget expenditures for the *entire previous budget period* in item 8a. Please separate expenditures into Federal grant funds and non-Federal funds (match/cost-share) expended for the project during the entire previous budget period.

     Note: If you are reporting on the first budget period of the project, leave item 8a. blank.

   - Report your actual budget expenditures for the *current budget period to date* (i.e., through 30 days before the due date of this report) in item 8b. Please separate expenditures into Federal grant funds and non-Federal funds (match/cost-share) expended for the project during the current budget period to date.

   --Final Performance Reports:

   - Report your actual budget expenditures for the *entire previous budget period* in item 8a. Please separate expenditures into Federal grant funds and non-Federal funds (match/cost-share) expended for the project during the entire previous budget period.

   - Report your actual budget expenditures for the *entire final budget period* in item 8b. Please separate expenditures into Federal grant funds and non-Federal funds (match/cost-share) expended for the project during the entire final budget period.

   - Report your actual budget expenditures for the *entire project period (performance period)* in item 8c. Please separate expenditures into Federal grant funds and non-Federal funds (match/cost-share) expended for the project during the entire project period. Your project period (performance period) start and end dates are found in Block 6 of the GAN.

9. **Indirect Costs**

   The indirect cost information requested in Items 9a. – 9d. must be completed by your Business Office.

   --Annual and Final Performance Reports:

   - Item 9a -- Please check "yes" or "no" in item 9a. to indicate whether or not you are claiming indirect costs under this grant.
   - Item 9b. -- If you checked "yes" in item 9a., please indicate in item 9b. whether or not your organization has an Indirect Cost Rate Agreement that was approved by the Federal government.
   - Item 9c. -- If you checked "yes" in item 9b., please indicate in item 9c. the beginning and ending dates covered by the Indirect Cost Rate Agreement. In addition, please indicate whether ED or another Federal

Figure 7–1a *continues*

agency (Other) issued the approved agreement. If you check "Other," please specify the name of the Federal agency that issued the approved agreement. *For final performance reports only*, check the appropriate box to indicate the type of indirect cost rate that you have – Provisional, Final, or Other. If you check "Other," please specify the type of indirect cost rate.

- Item 9d. – For grants under Restricted Rate Programs (EDGAR, 34 CFR 75.563), please indicate whether you are using a restricted indirect cost rate that is included on your approved Indirect Cost Rate Agreement or whether you are using a restricted indirect cost rate that complies with 34 CFR 76.564(c)(2). Note: State or Local government agencies may not use the provision for a restricted indirect cost rate specified in EDGAR, 34 CFR 76.564(c)(2). Check only one response. Leave blank, if this item is not applicable.

10. Annual Institutional Review Board (IRB) Certification

--Annual Performance Reports Only:

Annual certification is required if Attachment HS1, Continuing IRB Reviews, was attached to the GAN. Attach the IRB certification to the ED 524B as instructed in Attachment HS1.

11. Performance Measures Status

--Annual Performance Reports:

Please check "yes" or "no" in item 11a. to indicate whether *complete* data on performance measures for the current budget period are included in this report in Section A of the Project Status Chart. If no, please indicate in item 11b. the date when the information will be available and submitted to ED. Complete data must be submitted for any performance measures established by ED for the grant program (included in the attached "Dear Colleague Letter") and for any project specific performance measures that were included in your approved application.

If *complete* data on performance measures for the entire current budget period have not been obtained when you submit the ED 524B, please submit *available* data for the budget period to date with this report, unless instructed otherwise by your program office. *Complete performance measures data for the current budget period should be submitted by the date you indicated in item 11b.*

Note: Your program office will inform you of the *final date* by which performance measures data must be submitted to the Department for this program.

-- Final Performance Reports:

You must check "yes" in item 11a. Complete data on performance measures for the final budget period *must* be submitted with the final performance report in Section A of the Project Status Chart. Leave item 11b. blank.

Complete data *must* be submitted for any performance measures established by ED for the grant program (included in the attached "Dear Colleague Letter") and for any project-specific performance measures that were included in your approved grant application.

12. Certification

--Annual and Final Performance Reports:

The grantee's authorized representative must sign the certification for the ED 524B. If the grantee has any known internal control weaknesses concerning data quality (as disclosed through audits or other reviews), this information must be disclosed under Section C (Additional Information) of the Project Status Chart as well as the remedies taken to ensure the accuracy, reliability, and completeness of the data.

Figure 7–1a *continued*

INSTRUCTIONS FOR THE EXECUTIVE SUMMARY

--Annual and Final Performance Reports:

Provide a one to two page Executive Summary for *annual performance reports* and a two to three page Executive Summary for *final performance reports*. Provide highlights of the project's goals, the extent to which the expected outcomes and performance measures were achieved, and what contributions the project has made to research, knowledge, practice, and/or policy. Include the population served, if appropriate.

Note: The Executive Summary for *final performance reports* covers the **entire project period.**

INSTRUCTIONS FOR THE PROJECT STATUS CHART

General Instructions for Section A -- Project Objectives Information and Related Performance Measures Data

-- Annual and Final Performance Reports:

In your approved grant application, you established project objectives stating what you hope to achieve with your funded grant project. Generally, one or more performance measures were also established for each project objective that serve to demonstrate whether you have met or are making progress towards meeting each project objective. In addition to project-specific performance measures that you may have established in your approved grant application, performance measures may have been established by ED for the grant program [included in the attached "Dear Colleague Letter"] that you are required to report on.

In Section A of the Project Status Chart, you will report on the results to date of your project evaluation as required under EDGAR, 34 CFR 75.590. According to the instructions below, for each project objective included in your approved grant application, provide quantitative and/or qualitative data for each associated performance measure and a description of preliminary findings or outcomes that demonstrate that you have met or are making progress towards meeting the performance measure. You will also explain how your data on your performance measures demonstrate that you have met or are making progress towards meeting each project objective.

Note: Complete data *must* be submitted for any performance measures established by ED for the grant program (included in the attached "Dear Colleague Letter") and for any project-specific performance measures that were included in your approved grant application

For Annual Performance Reports: If *complete* data on performance measures for the entire current budget period have not been obtained when you submit the ED 524B, please submit *available* data for the budget period to date with this report, unless instructed otherwise by your program office. *Complete performance measures data for the current budget period should be submitted by the date you indicated in item 11b on the ED 524B Cover Sheet.* Your program office will inform you of the *final date* by which performance measures data must be submitted to the Department for this program.

For Final Performance Reports: Complete data on performance measures for the final budget period *must* be submitted with the final performance report.

For final performance reports, the information in Section A of the Project Status Chart covers the final budget period of the grant. Additional questions for final performance reports covering the entire project period are found in the instructions for Section C of the Project Status Chart.

Figure 7–1a *continues*

Instructions for Section A

- **Project Objective:**

Enter each project objective that is included in your approved grant application. Only one project objective should be entered per row. Project objectives should be numbered sequentially, i.e., 1., 2., 3., etc.

Update Box

If instructed by your program office in the attached "Dear Colleague Letter," please provide an update on the status of your project objectives for any period of time that you did not report on in your previous annual performance report.

Check the "Update Box" next to each project objective for which you are providing an update. Do not check the "Update Box" if you are reporting on a project objective for the current reporting period. If you are providing a status update on your project objectives for the previous budget period and reporting on those same objectives for the current reporting period, please use separate pages (Section A) to separate previous and current information. Do not combine information for the previous budget period and for the current reporting period on the same page.

Example: Last year's annual performance report covered 8 months of the previous budget period. The program office requests that you report on the status of your project objectives for the last 4 months of the previous budget period in this annual performance report.

- **Performance Measure:**

For each project objective, enter each associated performance measure. There may be multiple performance measures associated with each project objective. Enter only one performance measure per row. Each performance measure that is associated with a particular project objective should be labeled using an alpha indicator. Example: The first performance measure associated with project objective "1" should be labeled "1.a.," the second performance measure for project objective "1" should be labeled "1.b.," etc.

- **Measure Type:**

For each performance measure you are reporting on, enter the type of performance measure. Enter one (1) of the following measure types: **GPRA; PROGRAM; or PROJECT.**

The specific measures established by ED for the grant program that you are required to report on are included in the attached "Dear Colleague Letter." The measure type is also specified.

There are two types of measures that ED may have established for the grant program:

1. **GPRA:** Measures established for reporting to Congress under the Government Performance and Results Act; and
2. **PROGRAM:** Measures established by the program office for the particular grant competition.

In addition, report on any project-specific performance measures **(PROJECT)** that you, the grantee, established in your approved grant application to meet your project objectives.

- **Quantitative Data:**

Target and Actual Performance Data

Provide the target you established for meeting each performance measure and provide actual performance data demonstrating progress towards meeting or exceeding this target. Only quantitative (numeric) data should be entered in the Target and Actual Performance Data boxes.

The Target and Actual Performance Data boxes are each divided into three columns: **Raw Number; Ratio; and Percentage (%).**

For performance measures that are stated in terms of a single number (e.g., the number of workshops that will be conducted or the number of students that will be served), the target and actual performance data should be reported as a single number under the **Raw Number column** (e.g., **10** workshops or **80** students). Please leave the **Ratio and Percentage (%) columns** blank.

Figure 7–1a *continued*

For performance measures that are stated in terms of a percentage (e.g., percentage of students that attain proficiency), complete both the **Ratio column** and the **Percentage (%) column**. Please leave the **Raw Number column** blank.

In the **Ratio column** (e.g., **80/100**), the numerator represents the numerical target (e.g., the number of students that are expected to attain proficiency) or actual performance data (e.g., the number of students that attained proficiency), and the denominator represents the universe (e.g., all students served). Please enter the corresponding percentage (e.g., **80%**) in the **Percentage (%) column**.

If the collection of quantitative data is not appropriate for a particular performance measure, please leave the Target and Actual Performance Data boxes blank and provide an explanation and any relevant qualitative data for the performance measure in the block entitled, **Explanation of Progress**.

Note: If you are using weighted data, please indicate how the data are weighted in the block entitled, **Explanation of Progress.**

Special instructions for grants in their first budget period: If baseline data for a performance measure were not included in your approved application and targets were not set for the first budget period, then enter either the number **999** under the **Raw Number column** or the ratio **999/999** under the **Ratio column** of the **Target box**, depending on how your data will be reported in the future. The **999** or **999/999** indicates that baseline data are being collected on the measure during the first budget period and targets have not yet been set. Unless otherwise instructed by your program office in the attached "Dear Colleague Letter," report baseline data collected during the first budget period under either the **Raw Number column** or the **Ratio and Percentage (%) columns** of the **Actual Performance Data box**, as appropriate. After baseline data have been collected during the first budget period, grantees are expected to set targets for the second and any subsequent budget periods and report actual performance data in their annual performance reports.

- **Explanation of Progress (Includes Qualitative Data and Data Collection Information):**

  1. For each project objective and associated performance measures, indicate what data (quantitative and/or qualitative) were collected and when they were collected, the evaluation methods that were used, and how the data were analyzed. Clearly identify and explain any deviations from your approved evaluation plan, including changes in design or methodology, or the individual or organization conducting the evaluation.

  2. Based on your data, provide a description of preliminary findings or outcomes, including information to show whether you are making progress towards meeting each performance measure. Further, indicate how your performance measures data show that you have met or are making progress towards meeting the stated project objective. In your discussion, provide a brief description of your activities and accomplishments for the reporting period that are related to each project objective.

  3. If expected data were not attained, expected progress was not made toward meeting a performance measure or project objective, or a planned activity was not conducted as scheduled, provide an explanation. Include a description of the steps and schedules for addressing the problem(s) or issue(s).

  4. Indicate how you used your data and information from your evaluation to monitor the progress of your grant, and if needed, to make improvements to your original project plan (e.g., project activities and milestones) which are consistent with your approved objectives and scope of work.

Figure 7–1a *continues*

Instructions for Section B – Budget Information

-- **Annual and Final Performance Reports:**

- Report budget expenditure data in items 8a. – 8c. of the ED 524B Cover Sheet, as applicable. Please follow the instructions for completing items 8a. – 8c. included in this instruction sheet.

- For budget expenditures made with Federal grant funds, you must provide an explanation if funds have not been drawn down from GAPS to pay for the budget expenditure amounts reported in items 8a. – 8c of the ED 524B Cover Sheet.

- Provide an explanation if you *did not* expend funds at the expected rate during the reporting period.

- Describe any significant changes to your budget resulting from modification of project activities.

- Describe any changes to your budget that affected your ability to achieve your approved project activities and/or project objectives.

-- **Annual Performance Reports Only:**

- Do you expect to have any unexpended funds at the end of the current budget period? If you do, explain why, provide an estimate, and indicate how you plan to use the unexpended funds (carryover) in the next budget period.

- Describe any anticipated changes in your budget for the **next** budget period that require prior approval from the Department (see EDGAR, 34 CFR 74.25 and 80.30, as applicable).

Instructions for Section C – Additional Information

-- **Annual Performance Reports Only:**

- If applicable, please provide a list of current partners on your grant and indicate if any partners changed during the reporting period. Please indicate if you anticipate any change in partners during the next budget period. If any of your partners changed during the reporting period, please describe whether this impacted your ability to achieve your approved project objectives and/or project activities.

- *If instructed by your program office*, please report on any statutory reporting requirements for this grant program.

- Describe any changes that you wish to make in the grant's activities for the next budget period that are consistent with the scope and objectives of your approved application.

- If you are requesting changes to the approved key personnel listed in Block 4 of your GAN for the next budget period, please indicate the name, title and percentage of time of the requested key personnel. Additionally, please attach a resume or curriculum vitae for the proposed key personnel when you submit your performance report.

  Note: Do not report on any key personnel changes made during the current or previous budget period(s). Departmental approval must be requested and received prior to making key personnel changes.

- Provide any other appropriate information about the status of your project including any unanticipated outcomes or benefits from your project.

Figure 7–1a *continued*

-- Final Performance Reports Only:

(This information covers the entire project period.)

Note: All grantees submitting a final performance report must answer question 1. The attached "Dear Colleague Letter" specifies any additional questions that you must answer from the list below, if any.

1. Utilizing your evaluation results, draw conclusions about the success of the project and its impact. Describe any unanticipated outcomes or benefits from your project and any barriers that you may have encountered.

2. What would you recommend as advice to other educators that are interested in your project? How did your original ideas change as a result of conducting the project?

3. If applicable, describe your plans for continuing the project (sustainability; capacity building) and/or disseminating the project results.

4. Report on any statutory reporting requirements for this grant program.

Paperwork Burden Statement
According to the Paperwork Reduction Act of 1995, no persons are required to respond to a collection of information unless such collection displays a valid OMB control number. The valid OMB control number for this information collection is **1890 –0004**. The time required to complete this information collection is estimated to average 22 hours per response, including the time to review instructions, search existing data resources, gather the data needed, and complete and review the information collection. If you have any comments concerning the accuracy of the time estimate (s) or suggestions for improving this form, please write to: U. S. Department of Education, Washington, D.C. 2020-4651. If you have comments or concerns regarding the status of your individual submission of this form, write directly to (insert program office), U.S. Department of Education, 400 Maryland Avenue, S.W., Washington, D.C. 20202.

Figure 7–1a *continued*

U.S. Department of Education
Grant Performance Report Cover Sheet (ED 524B)

OMB No. 1890-0004

Check only one box per Program Office instructions.
☐ Annual Performance Report ☐ Final Performance Report

Expiration: 10-31-2007

General Information

1. PR/Award #: |_|_|_|_|_|_|_|_|_|_|_|
   (Block 5 of the Grant Award Notification.)

2. NCES ID #: |_|_|_|_|_|_|_|_|_|_|_|
   (See Instructions.)

3. Project Title: _____
   (Enter the same title as on the approved application.)

4. Grantee Name *(Block 1 of the Grant Award Notification.)*:_____

5. Grantee Address *(See Instructions.)*

6. Project Director Name:_____Title:_____
   Ph. #: (___) _____ - _____ Ext: (___) Fax #: (___) _____ - _____
   Email Address:_____

Reporting Period Information *(See instructions.)*

7. Reporting Period: From: ____/____/_____ To: ____/____/_____ (mm/dd/yyyy)

Budget Expenditures *(To be completed by your Business Office. See instructions. Also see Section B.)*

8. Budget Expenditures

	Federal Grant Funds	Non-Federal Funds *(Match/Cost Share)*
a. Previous Budget Period		
b. Current Reporting Period		
c. Entire Project Period *(For Final Performance Reports only)*		

Indirect Cost Information *(To be completed by your Business Office. See instructions.)*

9. Indirect Costs
   a. Are you claiming indirect costs under this grant? ___Yes ___No
   b. If yes, do you have an Indirect Cost Rate Agreement approved by the Federal government? ___Yes ___No
   c. If yes, provide the following information:
   Period Covered by the Indirect Cost Rate Agreement: From:____/____/____ To: ____/____/____ (mm/dd/yyyy)
   Approving Federal agency: _____ED _____Other *(Please Specify)*:_____
   Type of Rate *(For Final Performance Reports Only)*: ___Provisional ___Final ___Other *(Please specify)*_____
   d. For Restricted Rate Programs (check one) -- Are you using a restricted indirect cost rate that :
   _____ Is included in your approved Indirect Cost Rate Agreement?
   _____ Complies with 34 CFR 76.564(c)(2)?

Human Subjects *(See instructions.)*

10. Annual Certification of Institutional Review Board (IRB) Approval? ___Yes ___No ___N/A

Performance Measures Status and Certification *(See instructions.)*

11. Performance Measures Status
    a. Are complete data on performance measures for the current budget period included in the Project Status Chart? ___Yes ___No
    b. If no, when will the data be available and submitted to the Department? ____/____/_____ (mm/dd/yyyy)

12. To the best of my knowledge and belief, all data in this performance report are true and correct and the report fully discloses all known weaknesses concerning the accuracy, reliability, and completeness of the data.

Name of Authorized Representative:	Title:
Signature:	Date:

ED 524B

Page 1 of 5

Figure 7-1b *Instructions for grant reports.*
Source: United States Department of Education.

U.S. Department of Education
Grant Performance Report (ED 524B)
Executive Summary

OMB No. 1890 - 0004
Expiration: 10-31-2007

PR/Award #:

(See Instructions.)

ED 524B

Page 2 of 5

Figure 7–1b *continued*

U.S. Department of Education
Grant Performance Report (ED 524B)
Project Status Chart

OMB No. 1894-0003
Exp. 02/28/2011

PR/Award # (11 characters): _____

SECTION A - Performance Objectives Information and Related Performance Measures Data (See Instructions. Use as many pages as necessary.)

1. Project Objective   [ ] Check if this is a status update for the previous budget period.

1.a. Performance Measure	Measure Type	Quantitative Data						
		Target			Actual Performance Data			
		Raw Number	Ratio	%	Raw Number	Ratio	%	
			/			/		

1.b. Performance Measure	Measure Type	Quantitative Data						
		Target			Actual Performance Data			
		Raw Number	Ratio	%	Raw Number	Ratio	%	
			/			/		

Explanation of Progress (Include Qualitative Data and Data Collection Information)

ED 524B

Page 3 of 5

Figure 7–1c *Project status report.*
Source: United States Department of Education.

OMB No. 1894-0003
Exp. 02/28/2011

U.S. Department of Education
Grant Performance Report (ED 524B)
Project Status Chart

PR/Award # (11 characters): _____

SECTION A - Performance Objectives Information and Related Performance Measures Data (See Instructions. Use as many pages as necessary.)

2. Project Objective [ ] Check if this is a status update for the previous budget period.

2.a. Performance Measure	Measure Type	Quantitative Data							
		Target			Actual Performance Data				
		Raw Number	Ratio	%	Raw Number	Ratio	%		
			/			/			

2.b. Performance Measure	Measure Type	Quantitative Data							
		Target			Actual Performance Data				
		Raw Number	Ratio	%	Raw Number	Ratio	%		
			/			/			

Explanation of Progress (Include Qualitative Data and Data Collection Information)

ED 524B

Page 4 of 5

Figure 7–1c *continues*

OMB No. 1894-0003
Exp. 02/28/2011

U.S. Department of Education
Grant Performance Report (ED 524B)
Project Status Chart

PR/Award # (11 characters): _____

SECTION B - Budget Information (See Instructions. Use as many pages as necessary.)

SECTION C - Additional Information (See Instructions. Use as many pages as necessary.)

ED 524B

Page 5 of 5

Figure 7–1c *continued*

GRANT MANAGEMENT

NATIONAL ENDOWMENT FOR THE HUMANITIES

Performance Reporting Requirements

Formerly ENCLOSURE 2 - Revised July 1998
OMB No. 3136-0134, expires 6/30/09

The requirements in this document apply to MOST awards issued by NEH. Please refer to the "Remarks" section on the Official Notice of Action form of your award package to ensure that these requirements apply to your grant.

If you have questions concerning these grant requirements, they can be addressed to the grant administrator assigned to your grant, whose name appears in the award documents under "Endowment Administration of The Award." You can also reach the Office of Grant Management by telephone at 202/606-8494, or fax at 202/606-8633, or via the Internet at grantmanagement @neh.gov.

Enclosure 2 Performance Reporting Requirements

GENERAL REPORTING REQUIREMENTS

Grantees are required to submit a report of project accomplishments at the conclusion of the grant. Frequently, performance reports are also required during the course of a project. When events that have a significant impact on the project occur between scheduled performance reporting dates, these should be reported to the Endowment immediately.

If a grantee is required to submit interim performance reports, the due dates for these reports will be listed on the last page of the grant award. The final performance report is due within ninety days after the end of the grant period. (When a grantee has submitted an application for a continuation of a project, the appropriate Endowment program should be contacted to determine if the application may serve as a final report of accomplishment for the earlier grant.)

Two copies of each report should be submitted through the institutional grant administrator of the grantee organization (if applicable) and forwarded only to the

(continues)

Figure 7–2 *Instructions for grant reports.*
Source: National Endowment for the Humanities.

Office of Grant Management
Room 311
National Endowment for the Humanities
1100 Pennsylvania Avenue, N.W.
Washington, D.C. 20506.

PURPOSE OF REPORTS

Interim performance reports serve as a measure of progress achieved on a project and help to identify programmatic and administrative problems that may need to be resolved. Final performance reports become a permanent record of project accomplishments. These reports provide information that the Endowment staff uses to evaluate the significance and impact of NEH grants.

FORMAT OF REPORTS

Performance reports should be arranged as follows:

1. Cover Page
2. Narrative Description
3. Appendices (as needed)

1. COVER PAGE

Provide the following information in the order requested:

- type of report (interim or final performance report),
- grant number,
- title of project,
- name of project director(s),
- name of grantee institution (if applicable),
- date report is submitted.

2. NARRATIVE DESCRIPTION

The items listed are provided as guidance to the project director in developing the narrative description of project activities. Because projects vary considerably, not all items will be relevant to a particular project. Please feel free to organize this portion of the report in the way that most clearly presents what has taken place during the grant period.

Figure 7–2 *continued*

Interim Performance Reports

- Compare actual accomplishments with goals established for the report period. Whenever possible, describe the work accomplished in both quantitative and qualitative terms. If project goals have not been met, explain the reason for this, what steps have been taken to get the project back on schedule, and whether it seems likely that the project will be completed by the expiration date of the grant. Favorable developments that will enable project goals to be realized sooner or at less cost than anticipated should be described.
- Describe any changes that have been made or are anticipated in the project work plan or methodology.
- If the role of consultants, as outlined in the approved project plan, has changed, explain how and why it has changed.
- If applicable, describe how automation contributed to the project and whether hardware, software, or staffing problems have been encountered.
- If federal matching funds are a component of the award and the full amount of gifts has not yet been raised, provide information on ongoing fund-raising activities and the prospects for raising additional gifts.

The narrative description of an interim performance report should average between one and three pages in length.

Final Performance Report

Using the project description and plan of work that were approved by NEH as a point of departure, the final performance report should address the following subjects

a. Project Activities
  - Provide a description of the major activities that occurred during the grant period.
  - Indicate the reasons for omissions and changes in project activities.
  - If project performance was affected by changes in key project personnel, explain why the changes were made and how performance was affected.
  - When federal matching funds were a component of the award, summarize fund-raising experiences and the major factors believed to be responsible for success or failure in raising third-party support.
  - For projects involving computer applications, describe any changes that were made in the method of data entry, the specific data to be encoded, software, hardware, file systems, or search strategies.
  - Briefly describe any efforts that were made to publicize the results of the program.

Figure 7–2 *continues*

b. Accomplishments
- Compare the accomplishments of the project in quantitative and qualitative terms with the objectives proposed in the application.
- When project goals were not achieved, indicate what plans there are to complete the project after the grant period, how project activities will be funded, and when they are likely to be completed.

c. Audiences
- Describe the audiences for the project. Indicate the nature, size, geographic reach, sex, and age of the audience and assess the impact that the project had on this audience. What kinds of new or previously underserved audiences did the project attract? It is particularly important to compile quantitative information for this section of the report. Please include data on all screenings and broadcasts, if applicable.
- How much of an increase in visitor flow or membership did your organization experience as a result of the project?
- In the case of grants whose purpose was to affect a number of other institutions, include in the report a complete list of participants and appropriate statistical profiles that show the impact of the project by geographical region (if possible), kind of institution, and level and type of participant.

d. Evaluation
- Was an evaluation of the project performed? If so, briefly describe how the evaluation was performed and by whom.
- Describe the results of the evaluation and your own assessment of the program. Discuss both the weaknesses and the strengths of the program. A discussion that includes how problems were dealt with will be more helpful to NEH staff than one that focuses exclusively on the project's successes.
- How did the public respond to the project? What did they like or not like? What anecdotes, statistical summaries, feedback from Web sites, viewer remarks, or examples of media coverage can you provide that would help to assess the project's success?

e. Continuation of the Project
- Indicate if there are any plans to continue the project after the grant period because of the success of the program and the interest it has generated.
- When there was a commitment on the part of the grantee institution to continue a program after the grant period, explain how the commitment will be honored. If the program will not be continued, provide a detailed explanation for the change in plans.
- What kinds of new collaborative partnerships were formed (or strengthened) between your institution and other organizations (e.g., museums, historical societies, schools, universities, community groups, special interest groups, etc.) as a result of the project? Will these new partnerships continue and, if so, how?

f. Long-Term Impact
- What kinds of long-term impact (such as spin-off programs, use in the classroom or other indicators of continuing interest) will result from the project?

Figure 7–2 *continued*

- How did the project affect your institution's ability to attract additional non-federal financial support, either for the project or for activities that grew out of the project?
- What effect did the project have on the public's perception of your institution and on your plans for future projects?

g. Grant Products

- Indicate what grant products were produced during the course of the project and any future publication or distribution plans for materials resulting from grant activities.

Normally, the information that is to be included in a final narrative description can adequately be covered in a report that does not exceed ten typewritten pages.

3. APPENDICES

Enclose with the report one copy of any supporting material that would contribute to an understanding of the project and its accomplishments to date. This would include:

- representative samples of completed work,
- preliminary products such as conference or workshop papers,
- course syllabi and manuals,
- written evaluations of a project,
- consultant reports, if required,
- articles submitted to journals,
- illustrated field reports,
- copies of published announcements or other formal efforts to recruit participating scholars,
- copies of any mailing, fliers, newspaper releases or articles, or other media coverage.

It is not necessary to append work in progress, such as draft chapters of a book or other manuscript materials. However, unless otherwise specified in the conditions of the grant award, two copies of any publication, film, videotape, or slide presentation resulting from the grant should be forwarded to the Endowment with the final report.

OMB Required Burden Statement: NEH estimates the average time to complete this form is two hours per response. This estimate includes the time for reviewing instructions, researching, gathering, and maintaining the information needed; and completing and reviewing the final performance report. Please send any comments regarding this estimated completion time or any other aspect of this form, including suggestions for reducing completion time, to the Director, Office of Publications and Public Affairs, National Endowment for the Humanities, Washington, D.C. 20506; and to the Office of Management and Budget, Paperwork Reduction Project (3136-0134), Washington, D.C. 20503. According to the Paperwork Reduction Act of 1995, no persons are required to respond to a collection of information unless it displays a valid OMB control number.

Figure 7–2 *continued*

INSTITUTE *of*
Museumand**Library**
SERVICES

OMB No.: 3137-0029
Expiration Date: 01/31/07

Interim & Final Performance Reporting Instructions for IMLS Discretionary Awards

Reporting Requirements
All grantees are required to submit a report of project accomplishments within 90 days of the conclusion of a grant. Frequently, performance reports are also required during the course of a project. When events that have a significant impact on the project occur between scheduled narrative reporting dates, this <u>must</u> be reported to IMLS immediately.

If a grantee is required to submit one or more interim performance reports, the due dates for these reports will be listed on the Award Reporting Schedule which is attached to the Official Award Notification Document that is sent to both the project director and the authorizing official at the time the award is announced.

<u>Interim performance</u> reports usually run three to five pages.

<u>Final performance reports</u> cover the entire grant period and are normally longer than interim reports because, in addition to containing cumulative information on the outputs and outcomes of the project, the report is expected to provide an analysis of the overall achievements of the project and the value of grant products, a description of unanticipated events or circumstances that proved to be obstacles to project success, and a summary of the lessons that were learned during the course of the project. Three copies of any product resulting from grant activities, such as publications, research findings, software, workbooks, and other deliverables should be forwarded to IMLS with the final performance report or as they become available.

Reports of <u>20 pages or less</u> may be faxed (202-653-4604) or submitted electronically (<u>imlsreporting@imls.gov</u>).

Figure 7–3a *Instructions for grant reports.*
Source: Institute of Museum and Library Services.

Performance reports of <u>more than 20 pages</u> should be sent through the U.S. Postal Service or another delivery service to

> Grants Administration
> Institute of Museum and Library Services
> 1800 M Street, NW / 9th Floor
> Washington, DC 20036-5802

Performance Reports should be arranged as follows:

1. Cover Page
2. Performance Description
3. Certification Statement (at the end of Performance Description)
4. Appendices (as needed).

1. Cover Page

Provide the following information in the order requested:

Award Number _____
Awardee Institution Name_____
Indicate if the Report is an Interim or Final Report
Period Covered by the Report: From: _____ To: _____
Project Director Name and Title_____ _____
     Telephone_____ and E-mail _____

2. Performance Description

Please address the following questions and requests for information related to the progress achieved on the project during the reporting period.

a. What is the purpose of the project?

b. What activities or services have been carried out with project funds to support the purpose of the project? If the project schedule has not been met, explain why and describe the steps being taken to return the project to its proposed schedule of completion.

c. What are the outputs of the project activities or services to support the purpose of the project? Explain what documentation is used to report the outputs.

Figure 7–3a *continues*

d. What are the outcomes of the project activities or services to support the purpose of the project? Explain what documentation is used to report the outcomes.

e. Report other results of the project activities.

f. Additional comments/anecdotal information.

3. Certification (to be included at the end of Performance Description)
In submitting this report, I certify that all of the information is true and correct to the best of my knowledge.

Name and title of the person submitting the report and date of submission:

_____   _____ _____

Burden Estimate and Request for Public Comments
Public reporting burden for this collection of information is estimated to average one hour per response, including the time for reviewing instructions, searching existing data sources, gathering and maintaining the data needed, and completing and reviewing the collection of information. Send comment regarding this burden estimate or any other aspect of this collection of information, including suggestion for reducing this burden, to the Institute of Museum and Library Services, Chief, Information Officer, 1800 M Street, NW., 9th Floor, Washington, DC 20036-5802, and to the Office of Management and Budget, Paperwork Reduction Project (3137-0029), Washington, DC 20503.

Figure 7–3a *continued*

OMB No. 3137-0056
Expiration Date: 04/30/2008

Institute of Museum and Library Services
Native American Library Services
Basic Grant Final Financial and Performance Report

Use this format to submit your final financial and performance report for the IMLS Native American Library Services Basic Grant. File a separate report for each grant awarded; do not combine two or more grants onto one report form. Final reports are due ninety (90) days after the end of the grant period.

Grantee (Name of Tribe):
Grant number:
Amount of grant award: $
Name of Project Director:
Telephone number of Project Director:

Describe how the grant funds were used to support library and information services. The activities described should follow the categories identified in the spending plan approved when the grant was awarded (e.g., salaries and wages, books and journals, equipment and supplies). Please identify any significant differences between your approved spending plan and your actual expenditures of the grant funds. Any unspent funds must be returned.

Funds expended: $_____

Funds remaining (if any) *:   _____
            Total:

*to be returned to IMLS with Final Report; make check payable to IMLS

Name and title of person submitting this report (if different than Project Director):_____
Telephone number of person submitting this report: _____

By signing below, I certify that the information provided is true and correct and that all funds were used in accordance with the grant guidelines or returned to the Institute of Museum and Library Services.

Signature of person submitting this report: _____   Date: _____

You may either fax this report to IMLS Grants Administration at 202-653-4604 or mail it to Grants Administration; Institute of Museum and Library Services; 1800 M Street, NW / 9th Floor; Washington, DC 20036-5802.

Figure 7–3b *continues*

public funders, a grantee may find that several grant reports are due on the same date or within days of each other. The best way to handle this situation is to plan ahead and leave plenty of time to work on the reports.

It is critical that grant performance reports are submitted in a timely manner. Failure to do so could jeopardize the receipt of final funds. The reputation of a grantee can also be at stake. Those who are known for being poor grant managers may have an extremely difficult time getting continuation funding or even receiving a grant award from a new funder.

When creating a calendar, the staff person responsible for managing a grant should factor in the amount of time it may take to collect data and submit the report by the due date. If a grantee is working with a consortium of partners and must rely on them to provide specific data and information, additional time may be necessary to contact the partners and make the request.

Accurate Reporting

When a project does not go well, or if data are missing, it might be tempting to submit a report that contains misinformation. Grantees who are monitoring their projects on an ongoing basis should contact a program officer when problems or issues arise. Grantees should have a frank discussion with the program officer and offer strategies to solve the problems. Grant managers might also ask program officers for their advice about what steps to take to solve problems.

Chapter Summary

Managing federal grants can be a huge undertaking, especially for grantees with simultaneous grant management deadlines. Grantees should familiarize themselves with the corresponding OMB circulars associated with their grant. Grantees should also read the terms and conditions of the grant early in the project and create a calendar of report deadlines. Timeliness of report submission can affect the receipt of grant funds. The information in a grant report should always be as accurate as the grantee can make it.

Chapter 8

Managing Private Funder Grants

For the most part, there is no difference between the content of the reports that are required by private funders such as foundations and the reports required by the federal funders. Large national foundations, like the Robert Wood Johnson Foundation and the Kresge Foundation, have reporting requirements similar to those used by government funders. However, a review of the sample documents in this chapter will illustrate a major difference between public funders and smaller private funders like community and family foundations.

Difference in Complexity

As the sample report forms in this chapter illustrate, many private funders request a simple report from their grantees at the end of the project period. The Community Foundation of Central Florida combines the programmatic and fiscal information on one page (see **Figure 8–1**). Grantees are encouraged to use an extra sheet of paper only if it is necessary to respond to the questions. The Southeastern Minnesota Arts Council also combines the information and also encourages the use of another sheet of paper, if necessary (see **Figure 8–2**). The Champlin Foundations use a one-page form as the final financial report for the grant as well as interim reports for a multi-year grant (see **Figure 8–3**). The Lancaster Emergency Medical Services Association's 90-day report to the Lancaster County Foundation could not be any simpler (see **Figure 8–4**).

C O M M U N I T Y F O U N D A T I O N
of Central Florida
FINAL EVALUATION

INSTRUCTIONS

The Community Foundation of Central Florida is committed to evaluating all of the programs and projects it funds in order to assess its effectiveness in the community. This form is to be filled out (use separate sheet if necessary) upon completion of the grant requirements, signed by your agency's executive director and board chair, and returned to the Community Foundation at the address provided at the bottom of the page.

EVALUATION

Name of Organization: _____

Address: _____ Email: _____

City, State, Zip: _____ Phone: _____

Person Submitting Evaluation: _____
　　　　　　　　　　　　　　　　　　　Name　　　　　　　　　　　　　　　　　　Title

Date Project Funded: _____/ _____/ _____ 　Amount Awarded: $_____

1. Please explain in narrative form how this grant aided your organization in "Capacity Building."

2. Give examples of specific outcomes produced from the use of this money, with reference to the definition of "Capacity Building." What was the value added component to the use of this money? (demographics and #'s of services provided)

3. Provide complete financial detail documenting how the money was spent. (Documentation is not required)
    Dates Disbursed　　　　　Amounts　　　　　To Whom　　　　　Purpose

4. The Community Foundation requires public recognition of funding. Please detail any publicity naming the Foundation as a donor. Attach copies of news releases, articles, etc. (paid advertising is not appropriate acknowledgement)

SIGNATURE

This form must be reviewed and signed by the organization's executive director and board chair.

_____　　_____
Executive Director　　　　　　Date　　　　Board Chair　　　　　　Date

1411 Edgewater Drive, Ste. 203, Orlando, FL 32804; ph. 407-872-3050; fx. 407-425-2990; web. www.cfcflorida.org

Figure 8–1 *Final report.*

Source: *Reprinted with permission of the Community Foundation of Central Florida.*

SEMAC Final Report Form
(Type in Black Ink. Do not change the format of this form.)

SOUTHEASTERN MINNESOTA ARTS COUNCIL, INC. (SEMAC)
1610 14th Street NW #206, Rochester, Minnesota 55901 (507) 281-4848, Fax (507) 281-8373
Serving Dodge, Fillmore, Freeborn, Goodhue, Houston, Mower, Olmsted, Rice, Steele, Wabasha, and Winona Counties

1. Grant Recipient (name, address & phone) :

2. Grant Number and one sentence description of project:

3. Please fill in the date, location and attendance for each activity included in the project. If there is not enough room provided, attach a separate sheet of information in the same format.

DATE   ACTIVITY   LOCATION   ATTENDANCE

TOTAL ATTENDANCE: _____

4.   Describe the project, being sure to include how it may have differed from the original proposal.

5. List the original stated goals of the project. How did you evaluate the acheivement of these goals? What were the results of your evaluation?

(continues)

Figure 8–2 *Final report.*

Source: Reprinted with permission of the Southeastern Minnesota Arts Council.

6. Describe the publicity for the project and how the SEMAC grant you received was acknowledged. (Attach representative samples of publicity materials)

7. Describe how your project was ADA (Americans with Disabilities Act) accessible.

8. Financial Report

COSTS	Proposed Budget		Actual Project Costs	
	Cash	In-Kind	Cash	In-Kind
1. Salaries				
2. Artist Fees				
3. Supplies & Materials				
4. Travel				
5. Publicity				
6. Rental & Other				
Subtotals				
Total Cost (Cash + In-Kind)				

INCOME	Proposed Budget	Actual Project Income
1. Carry-over Capital (cash on hand)		
2. Cash donations		
3. Non-SEMAC Grants		
4. Earned Income		
5. SEMAC Grant		
Total Income		

SURPLUS

Surplus / Profit amount $ _____ . If your project generated more income than your original proposal indicated, how will you designate these additional funds?

9. Letter of thanks sent to Legislative/Senate representative:

Yes _____   No _____   Representative(s) _____

I certify that the information contained in this report is true and correct to the best of my knowledge:

_____   _____   _____   _____
SIGNATURE   TYPED NAME   TITLE   DATE

Figure 8–2 *continued*

Why are the forms in these examples so simple to complete compared to the reports shown in Chapter 7? Reasons are probably related to government regulations, the size of the grantor foundation, and the size of the grant award.

Federal grant programs are created by legislation and come with regulations that must be followed for the administration of the grant. The OMB circulars described in Chapter 6 are examples of the type of government-wide policy that affects all federal

---

THE CHAMPLIN FOUNDATIONS
ANNUAL USE OF FUNDS REPORT

Organization:

Telephone:

Date of Grant Award:

Original Amount of Grant:

(A)Beginning Unspent Balance of Grant:

Amount Spent During this Period:

Date	Payee	Item	Amount

(B)Total Amount Spent During the Period

Ending Balance of Grant Remaining (A)-(B)

I hereby certify that I am authorized by the above organization to make this report and further certify that the above information is true and accurate to the best of my knowledge.

Signature: Date:

Print Name: Title:

Please use this form to submit your report detailing how grant dollars received
from these Foundations were spent during this reporting period.
REPORT EACH GRANT SEPARATELY
Reports are due annually, beginning December 31st in the year following the year of award,
until the entire grant has been expended.
Submit Reports Annually by December 31st to:
The Champlin Foundations ~ 300 Centerville Road, Suite 300S ~ Warwick, RI 02886-0226
TIMELY AND ACCURATE REPORTING IS MANDATORY IN ACCORDANCE WITH IRS REGULATIONS.
FAILURE TO COMPLY WILL ADVERSELY IMPACT ANY FUTURE APPLICATIONS.

Figure 8–3 *Use of funds report.*

Source: Reprinted with permission of the Champlin Foundations.

LEMSA

Lancaster Emergency Medical Services Association

The Lancaster County Foundation
90-Day Progress Report

What progress have you made in achieving the objectives of your program/project in the past 90-days?

    o   LEMSA took delivery of a 2003 Ford (Vartanian by Accubuilt) Wheel Chair Van on November 17, 2003. During the following weeks, the Van had wheelchair mounts, a two-way radio, and mud flaps installed. Additionally , the rear windows were tinted to allow for patient privacy. The Van was placed in-service on December 8, 2003.

What internal and/or external factors have contributed to or impeded the progress of your program/project in the past 90-days?

    o   There was no impedance.

Do you anticipate any difficulties completing your project in the timeframe outlined in your grant request?

    o   We did not.

Can the Foundation provide any assistance to ensure the successful completion of your program/project?

    o   Non-applicable – Van in service serving (on average) ten patients daily.

Figure 8–4 *Final report for the Lancaster Community Foundation.*
Source: *Reprinted with permission of Lancaster Emergency Medical Services Association.*

grant programs. Foundations, on the other hand, can be created by families, community members, and corporations. They are not governed by the same rules and regulations that federal funders are. In addition, there are differences in accountability for public and private funders. Public funders have grant programs made up of taxpayers' dollars and are held accountable to all of the U.S. taxpayers. Foundations, on the other hand, are often accountable to smaller groups like families (who account for the wealth of the foundation, community donors, or corporate stakeholders). Public funders are expected to show that the federal awards are being used appropriately and that the funded projects are having a positive impact.

Many foundations, especially small ones, only have one or two staff members available (some only on a part-time basis) to review grantee reports. In addition, the amount of the grant award may be small (a few thousand dollars, for example) compared to the size of the awards from federal funders. This often means that the scope of projects submitted to private funders can be smaller than those submitted to public funders. To be fair to grantees, shorter and simpler forms are required.

Additional Flexibility

Grantees may find that some private funders, due to their size and lack of regulations, may be more flexible than government funders. For example, deadlines for reports might be extended for mitigating circumstances. Or funders may provide the entire amount of the grant award at the beginning of the project and expect to receive reports accounting for the expenditure of the funds later in the project.

Chapter Summary

Generalizations about private funder grants cannot be made, as each of these funders has its own reporting requirements compared to federal funders. However, some private funders have much simpler forms for grantees to complete and have more flexibility in their interactions with grantees.

Chapter 9

Closeout Procedures

Grantees are required to close out their grants by both private and public funders. However, the term is usually only used by federal funders. A grant is ready to be closed out when all project activities have been carried out and all of the expenses associated with the project have been paid. Closing out a grant involves submitting all final reports required by the funder, a final financial report of all project costs and expenditures, and any additional forms or documents that the funder requires.

Grantees should read the terms and conditions to find out when the final reports must be submitted. Funders usually allow at least 30 days and some up to 90 days after the project is completed for the reports to be turned in.

Included in this chapter are samples of the information required in the closeout report for the National Institute of Occupational Safety and Health (see **Figure 9–1**), the Gaining Early Awareness and Readiness for Undergraduate Programs grant from the U.S. Department of Education (see **Figure 9–2**), and the Workforce Housing Reward Grant Program of the California Department of Housing and Community Development (see **Figure 9–3**). An example of a final report for the Lancaster County Foundation can be found in Chapter 8 (see Figure 8–4).

AWARD CLOSEOUT GUIDANCE
Grants and Cooperative Agreements Supported by
National Institute for Occupational Safety and Health
Centers for Disease Control and Prevention

1 October 2007

Centers for Disease Control and Prevention, National Institute for Occupational Safety and Health (CDC//NIOSH) will close out a grant as soon as possible after expiration of a grant that will not be extended or after termination of a grant as provided in 45 CFR 74.71 to 74.73. Grantees are required to submit the Closeout Report comprised of the three Final Reports described below within 90 days of the project end date. This date is on the notice of grant award, and can also be obtained from recipient Institution's business office. Failure to submit timely and accurate final reports may affect future funding to the Institution or awards for the same Principal Investigator (PI).

If the final reports cannot be submitted within 90 days, a written request and justification for an extension of the expiration date at least 10 days prior to the expiration date (per the HHS Grants Policy Statement) must be submitted. Otherwise, there is no guarantee that the extension request can be processed in time. The request must be sent to your Grants Management Specialist at the Procurement and Grants Office (PGO) address listed under Contacts at the end of this document. The PI should follow-up to verify that the request has been received by CDC Procurement and Grants Office (PGO.)

The NIOSH/Office of Extramural Programs (OEP) and CDC/PGO have prepared the following instructions to facilitate preparation of Closeout Reports by the PI and Business Office. These instructions, however, do not replace or supersede any Health and Human Services or CDC policy.

The reports required to closeout a completed award are: a) Final Progress Report; b) Final Financial Status Report; and c) Final Invention Statement. All reports must be sent directly to your CDC/PGO Grants Management Specialist identified in your Notice of Grant Award. A paper original, two (2) copies, and an electronic copy are requested.

Closeout Reports:

a) Final Progress Report
The Final Progress Report represents the most important report a PI prepares for a grant. It should communicate the results of the research and provide a synthesis of the overall project. NIOSH uses it as a principal reporting tool to inform the Congress, Executive Branch, NIOSH Director, and other stakeholders on the success and impact of the NIOSH extramural research program in addressing occupational safety and health issues. Thus, NIOSH relies on the PI to provide a cogent, well-organized report of findings that can be understood by a broad audience.

Although there is currently no standard Final Progress Report format, NIOSH and CDC/PGO have developed the following guidance for preparing final progress reports.

Title Page. The title page should contain the PI's name, affiliation and contact information (address, telephone, email); the institution to which the award was made (include full address); project title; date and number of report (if any); co-investigators, project director and sponsors; grant number(s); and the starting and ending dates.

Table of Contents.

List of Terms and Abbreviations.

Abstract. This is an overview of the project limited to no more than two pages (preferably one page) stating the occupational safety and health issue that was addressed, the importance of the problem, approach, key findings, and how the results can be utilized in the workplace. This section may contain

Figure 9–1 *Closeout report requirements.*
Source: *National Institute of Occupational Safety and Health.*

much of the same information as in the sections below, but it is intended to be a brief summary for informing others about the key findings and importance of the project. The abstract should be a stand-alone document that is suitable for distribution to a wide audience. The PI should realize that NIOSH/OEP may provide the Abstract to members of Congress, the Secretary of Health and Human Services, the Director of the Institute, and many others. Abstracts are often used without subsequent editing, however, the PI may be contacted directly if any clarifications are needed.

Highlights/Significant Findings. Highlights and/or significant findings are similar to conclusions. These are the important results of the project, and should relate to the specific aims of the project. The most important findings should be listed first. Separate findings should be in different paragraphs. Details can be placed in the Scientific Report section of the final report (below).

Translation of Findings. This section provides an interpretation of how the significant findings of the project can be used to prevent workplace diseases and injuries. If specific recommendations are made for reducing hazards on the job, the language should be as non-technical as possible to communicate to employers or employees. It is very important that a PI identify how these findings have been or may be adopted in the workplace. If the findings cannot yet be applied to the workplace, this section should address how these findings can be used to guide future investigative activities.

Outcomes/Relevance/Impact. This section summarizes, or otherwise concisely states the findings. The primary goal is to answer questions such as "How did this project lead to improvements in occupational safety and health?" or "How can the findings of this study guide future investigations and research?" This section is very important to NIOSH and may be used frequently in communications about your project. It is important to consider how your project relates to occupational safety and health with regard to improved practices, prevention/intervention techniques, legislation, policy, and use of technology. Important outcomes should be explained and classified in one of the following ways: 1) potential outcomes – findings, results, or recommendations that could impact workplace risk if used; 2) intermediate outcomes - how findings, results, or recommendations have been used by others to influence practices, legislation, product design, and so forth; and 3) end outcomes - how findings, results, or recommendations have contributed to documented reductions in work-related morbidity, mortality, and/or exposure.

Scientific Report. This report should contain the following: background for the project, specific aims, procedures, methodology, results and discussion, and conclusions. More detail should be provided in this section than is included in the "Significant Findings" section. Each of the specific aims originally planned or added during the project should be addressed in terms of what was accomplished or why progress was not made. In this way there will be a complete documentation of the efforts on the grant. **Information that is considered proprietary** for commercial purposes should be clearly noted as such in case a Freedom of Information Act (FOIA) request is received. Otherwise, the entire report may be released.

Publications. List the published or "in press" articles resulting from the grant support (NIOSH should be acknowledged in the articles). Provide annotations that describe how the articles relate to the specific aims. **Do not submit reprints or manuscripts.** In addition, investigators are encouraged to inform NIOSH about publications resulting from the project after the final report is submitted.

Citation Format Examples

Journal Articles
Clark WW, Popelka GR: [1989] Hearing Levels of Railroad Trainmen. Laryngoscope 99:1151-1157.

Gomes M, Santella RM: [1990] Immunologic Methods for the Detection of Benzo(a)pyrene Metabolites in Urine. Chemical Research in Toxicology, in press.

Books
Trush MA, Thompson DC: [1989] Enhancement of Chemical Activation Via Radical-Dependent Mechanisms: An Emerging Concept in Chemical-Chemical Interactions. In:

Figure 9–1 *continues*

Oxygen Radicals in Biology and Medicine, (eds. MG Simic, KA Taylor, JF Ward, CV Sonntag), Plenum Publishing Corporation, pp 739-744.

Murlas CG: [1989] Environmental Airway of Mucosal and Changes in Hyperreactivity. In Airway Epithelium: Structure and Function in Health and Disease, (eds. S Farmer, D Hay), Marcel Decker Inc., in press.

Proceedings
Park MY, Casali JG: [1989] A Laboratory Simulation of Selected In-field Influences on Hearing Protector Performance. Proc of 1989 Human Factors Society 33rd Annual Conference, Denver, Colorado, 946-950, October 16-20.

Dissertation/Thesis
Holton PM: [1986] Particle Size-Dependent leakage through the Face seal of Negative Pressure Half-Mask Respirators, Ph.D. Thesis, University of Cincinnati.

Inclusion of gender and minority study subjects. If applicable, use the gender and minority inclusion table provided in the PHS-2590.

Inclusion of Children. Where appropriate, indicate whether children were involved in the study or how the study was relevant for conditions affecting children. You can refer to the following internet sites http://grants1.nih.gov/grants/funding/children/children.htm http://grants.nih.gov/grants/funding/phs398/phs398.html.

Materials available for other investigators. Describe any data, research materials (such as cell lines, DNA probes, animal models), protocols, software, or other information resulting from the research that are available to be shared with other investigators and how it may be accessed.

b) Final Financial Status Report Forms. The institution's business office will determine whether the long form, SF-269 or the short form, SF-269A should be used for the Financial Status Report (FSR). Follow the instructions provided. Please provide an original and two (2) copies.

For organizations receiving their funds through the Health and Human Services Payment Management System (PMS), final reports, as specified by PMS, must be submitted to that office. It is the responsibility of the grantee to reconcile reports submitted to PMS and to the CDC awarding office.

Requirement. Final FSRs are required for grants that have been completed and are being closed, and grants that have expired or have been terminated. Final FSRs are also required when grants are transferred to a new grantee or are modified during the project and require an adjustment of funds. These include awards which will not be competitively extended through award of a new competitive segment.

Process.
The final FSR must:
- cover the period of time since the previous FSR submission or as much of the competitive segment as has been funded prior to termination;

- have no unliquidated obligations. Unliquidated obligations on a cash basis are obligations incurred, but not yet paid. On an accrual basis, they are obligations incurred, but for which an outlay has not yet been recorded; and

- indicate the exact balance of unobligated funds. Unobligated funds must be returned to CDC/PGO or must be reflected by an appropriate accounting adjustment in accordance with instructions from the GMO or from the payment office.

Figure 9–1 *continued*

Withdrawal of the unobligated balance following expiration or termination of a grant is not considered an adverse action and may not be appealed. Where the submission of a revised final FSR results in additional claims by the grantee, CDC will consider the approval of such claims subject to the following minimum criteria:

- the charges must represent allowable costs under the provisions of the grant;
- there must have been an unobligated balance for the given budget period that is sufficient to cover the additional claim. Such a claim may be considered regardless of whether the unobligated balance was moved forward to offset the award for a subsequent budget period;
- funds must be available from the applicable appropriation; and
- CDC/PGO must receive the revised FSR within 15 months of its due date.

c) Final Invention Statement and Certification Form.

Process. Final Invention Statement (HHS Form 568 - Fillable) signed by the PI and the institution's authorized official must be submitted even if there were no inventions. You must list all inventions conceived, or first actually reduced to practice, during the course of work under the project, from the original effective date of support through the date of expiration or termination, regardless if reported previously reported. If there were no inventions, indicate "None" on the statement.

CONTACTS:

Send original and two hard copies and an electronic copy to the Grants Management Specialist identified in your Notice of Grant Award.

For questions, contact:

CDC/PGO – Mr. Larry Guess, e-mail lguess@cdc.gov; telephone 412-386-6826

NIOSH/OEP – Your Scientific Program Administrator (identified in the Notice of Grant Award)

NIOSH/OEP — email OEPCorrespond@cdc.gov; telephone 404-498-2530

Figure 9–1 *continued*

OMB Approval No: 1840-0782
Expiration Date: 08/31/08

U.S. DEPARTMENT OF EDUCATION
Gaining Early Awareness and Readiness for Undergraduate Programs
(GEAR UP)

Financial Status And Program Performance Closeout Report
For State and Partnership GEAR UP Grants

COVER SHEET

1. PR/Award Number: _____

   (Located in block 5 of your grant award notification)

2. Name of Grantee: _____

3. Address: _____

4. Name of Project Director/Contact Person: _____

   Phone Number: _____   Fax: _____

   E-mail Address: _____

5. Name of Certifying Official: _____

   Phone Number: _____ E-mail Address: _____

6. Report Period: (e.g., Sept. 1, 1999 to Aug 31, 2004)

We certify that to the best of our knowledge, the information reported herein is accurate and complete.

_____   _____
Name of Project Director (Print)   Name of Certifying Official (Print)

_____   _____
Signature and Date   Signature and Date

According to the Paperwork Reduction Act of 1995, no persons are required to respond to a collection of information unless it displays a valid OMB control number. The valid OMB control number for this information collection is 1840-**XXXX**. The time required to complete this information collection is estimated to average **35** hours per response, including the time to review instructions, search existing data sources, gather the data needed, and complete and review the information collection. **If you have any comments concerning the accuracy of the time estimate(s) or suggestions for improving this form, please write to: U.S. Department of Education, Washington, DC 20202-4651. If you have comments or concerns regarding the status of your individual submission of the form, write directly to: The GEAR UP Program, U.S. Department of Education, 1990 K Street, N.W., Suite 6101, Washington, DC 20006-8524.**

Figure 9–2 *Closeout report requirements.*

Source: Gaining Early Awareness and Readiness for Undergraduate Programs, U.S. Department of Education.

INSTRUCTIONS:

In accordance with 34 CFR Section 75.590 (§75.590) of the Education Department General Administrative Regulations (EDGAR), all grant recipients are required to submit a final performance report. Before we can officially close out your grant, you must submit a final performance report to us by no later than 90 days after the grant expires.

This set of forms is the Financial Status and Program Performance Closeout Report for GEAR UP State and Partnership projects (hereafter cited as Closeout Report). A Closeout Report is used by the Department of Education to determine whether recipients of discretionary grants have made substantial progress towards meeting the objectives of their respective projects, as outlined in their grant applications and/or subsequent work plans. In addition, the final report allows the Department of Education to evaluate each grant project's fiscal operations for the entire grant performance period, and compare total expenditures relative to federal funds awarded, and actual cost-share/matching relative to the total amount in the approved grant application. The GEAR UP Closeout Report is also used to collect data addressing the performance of the program on a national level and thereby includes information for the Department to use when reporting outcome data regarding the GEAR UP performance indicators under the Government Performance and Results Act of 1993 (GPRA).

The Closeout Report consists of a cover sheet and six sections. The cover sheet must be completed and signed by the Project Director (or designated representative, if need be) and the certifying official and returned to the Department of Education along with the six sections on or before the due date. A copy of these forms and instructions will be mailed to each recipient of a GEAR UP grant that is in its final year of its performance period and will no longer be receiving federal funding for its GEAR UP program at the end of the current project year. Grantees are expected to complete all questions in the report. Please write "Not Applicable" or "N/A" if a question does not pertain to your project.

Unless otherwise noted, please provide information for the Closeout Report that is in accordance with the duration of your GEAR UP grant, such as a 5-year or 6-year performance period.

The final program performance and financial status reports are reviewed by the GEAR UP staff to ensure that grant recipients have achieved the goals of the GEAR UP grant program, are reporting information that demonstrates successful achievement of expected outcomes, and are in compliance with applicable Department regulations. Thus, please note: the final program performance and financial report review will determine if the GEAR UP grant is ready to be closed in "good standing" or needs to remain open for further departmental postaward action. If the report has not been received or the information in the report does not demonstrate successful achievement of expected outcomes, the Department of Education issues a noncompliance letter to the particular grant recipient.

We strongly encourage you to draw down on funds necessary to cover costs incurred while implementing the grant and meet the cost share/matching on approved budgets by no later than 90 days after the grant expires (December 1, 2005). Please note that any obligations incurred after August 31, 2005 cannot be charged to the grant.

Once we have determined that all of the closeout requirements and all other terms/conditions of your grant award have been met, we will send an official closeout notification to you.

Figure 9–2 *continues*

SECTION I: EXECUTIVE SUMMARY

Please describe the extent to which you have implemented all program activities and components planned for your grant. Highlight your major outcomes, successes, and concerns.

Figure 9–2 *continued*

SECTION II: NARRATIVE INFORMATION

Please address the following questions:

1) What aspects of your program do you think are most successful (have the greatest impact)? Why?

2) What barriers or problems have you encountered in administering your grant, and how have you addressed these problems?

3) Please describe the progress your project has made towards accomplishing the proposed objectives of your project as outlined in your grant application or subsequent workplans (i.e., describe the extent of making "substantial progress" towards meeting the project objectives and achieving the goals of the GEAR UP program).

In the table below, please list your Year 1 – Year 6 objectives, and indicate what activities took place with respect to each of these objectives, as well as the results of those activities.

Objectives: List the approved objectives from your grant application or work plan. Where applicable, provide baseline data.	Activities: List the activities that have been conducted to meet the objective.	Results: Has the objective been met? If not, why not and what progress have you made in reaching the objective?
Example: 1. Enrollment in 7th grade pre-algebra, 8th grade algebra, and 8th grade advanced science classes will increase by 5% each project year. Baseline: Pre-algebra 7th grade -- 10% Algebra 8th grade -- 5% Advanced Science 8th grade -- 20%	Example: Instructional support services, staff development to improve instruction, and articulation with elementary schools	Example: Enrollment changes from 2000/01 to 2001/02: 1) 7th grade pre-algebra: +65% 2) 8th grade algebra: +5% 3) 8th grade advanced science: -6% (due to increased standards for enrollment).
1.		
2.		
3.		
4.		
5.		

Figure 9–2 *continues*

4) What are some of the "lessons learned" from operating your GEAR UP project? That is, if GEAR UP was now in Year 1, what would you do differently?

5) What is the effect of your GEAR UP project on participants' academic achievement/ performance and preparation for postsecondary education (i.e., the impact of your project on those served)?

6) Describe how your project's activities and outcomes are likely to be sustained over time. Describe the systemic changes that have occurred in your school(s).

7) Please explain any other matter that you need to address or just want to share with the U.S. Department of Education, that would be helpful to the Department in evaluating your performance or understanding the contents of your closeout report.

Figure 9–2 *continued*

SECTION III: GRANT ADMINISTRATION INFORMATION

1) Please describe any significant changes in your project design since the approval of your grant application (*e.g.*, changing from individual tutoring to group tutoring or placing more emphasis on enrichment activities rather than remediation). How did these changes affect your budget, federal expenditures, or matching contributions?

2) Please describe any changes to the roles of your partners during the six years of your project. Describe any partners who have been added to your grant since the onset. Did the role of any of your partners in your final project year change significantly since they initially served your project? Did any partner(s) discontinue their participation in your grant?

3) If your project has a scholarship component for postsecondary education, please provide: a) information about the amount of scholarship money (federal and/or matching funds) that has been obligated; b) information regarding where scholarship funds are held pending distribution to former GEAR UP students (*e.g.*, are the funds in a trust account?); and c) how the funds will be disbursed and to whom. If you have already disbursed scholarship money to students, please indicate the amount of money disbursed, the number of students who received scholarships, and the average amount of the scholarships awarded.

Figure 9–2 *continues*

SECTION IV: DEMOGRAPHIC DATA

Demographic Data: Please complete the following tables requesting demographic data on GEAR UP students.

A. Students Served: Please complete the following table indicating the number of students served by your project.

	Number of Students
Number of students you proposed to serve during the grant period (total years 1-6)	
Actual number of students in your cohort(s) during the first year of your GEAR UP project	
Actual number of students in your cohort(s) during the second year of your GEAR UP project	
Actual number of students in your cohort(s) during the third year of your GEAR UP project	
Actual number of students in your cohort(s) during the fourth year of your GEAR UP project	
Actual number of students in your cohort(s) during the fifth year of your GEAR UP project	
Actual number of students in your cohort(s) during the sixth year of your GEAR UP project	

B. Participant Distribution by Ethnic Background: The following table regarding the ethnic background of GEAR UP students is not mandatory, but is extremely helpful to the Department of Education in reporting on the ethnic characteristics of students served by the program. The race/ethnicity categories used in this section are consistent with the Department of Education's policy on the collection of racial and ethnic information. These categories are defined as follows:

American Indian or Alaska Native – A person having origins in any of the original peoples of North America, and who maintains cultural identification through tribal affiliations or community recognition.

Asian – A person having origins in any of the original peoples of the Far East, Southeast Asia, and the Indian subcontinent. This area includes, for example, China, India, Japan, Korea, and the Philippine Islands.

Black or African American – A person having origins in any of the black racial groups of Africa.

Hispanic or Latino – A person of Mexican, Puerto Rican, Cuban, Central or South American, or other Spanish culture or origin, regardless of race.

White – A person having origins in any of the original peoples of Europe, North Africa, or the Middle East.

Native Hawaiian or Other Pacific Islander – A person having origins in any of the original peoples of Hawaii or other pacific islands such as Samoa and Guam.

Figure 9–2 *continued*

Please report on the actual number of students in your cohort(s) during the entire performance period (i.e., number of students served). This number may be different from the number served in the final year, because some students may have moved or dropped out in earlier years. Please note: If this number is not available, indicate the number served in the final project year of your project.

Ethnicity:	Number of GEAR UP Students
American Indian or Alaska Native	
Asian	
Black or African American	
Hispanic or Latino	
White	
Native Hawaiian or Other Pacific Islander	
Total	

Figure 9–2 *continues*

SECTION V: GEAR UP STUDENT OUTCOMES

This section of the report requests outcome information for the students you served during the entire performance period of your GEAR UP project. Please base your responses on information that is relevant at termination date of your GEAR UP project. These student academic achievement data are directly linked to the performance measures and outcome data that are part of GEAR UP's GPRA Performance Indicators.

1) **Cumulative Course Completion:** Please complete the following table indicating the number of GEAR UP students from the 9th, 10th, 11th, and/or 12th grades in your final project year, who successfully completed the courses identified.

The names for math classes can vary among schools. Classify courses based on the content of the course. "Advanced Placement" classes are courses designed to prepare students for the Advanced Placement Exams. *Optional:* If your cohort has changed significantly over time, and you would like to provide information about your original cohort, you may (but are not required to) provide information about students in your original cohort in parentheses after or below the numbers provided for the current cohort.

	9th Grade	10th Grade	11th Grade	12th Grade	Total Number of Students
Number of students in your final project year					
Number of students who completed Pre-Algebra by the end of 7th grade					
Number of students who completed Pre-Algebra by the end of 8th grade (would include those who completed Pre-Algebra by the end of earlier grades as well)					
Number of students who completed Algebra I by the end of 8th grade					
Number of students who completed Algebra I by the end of 9th grade (would include those who completed Algebra I by the end of earlier grades as well)					
Number of students who completed Algebra II					
Number of students who completed Geometry					
Number of students who completed any mathematics course above Geometry, not including Advanced Placement courses					
Number of students who completed Calculus					
Number of students who completed Chemistry					
Number of students who completed Physics					
Total					

Figure 9–2 *continued*

Example: The data element in Row 2, Column 1 would pertain to the number of the 9th graders in your final project year who completed Pre-Algebra by the end of their 7th grade. Column 2 would pertain to the number of 10th graders in your final project year who completed Pre-Algebra by the end of their 7th grade.

2) **High School Graduation:** What was the number of 12th graders during 2004-05 (students scheduled to graduate from high school in 2005/"Class of 2005")? (This number should equal the number of 12th grade students indicated in Row 1 on the above table.)

Please note: If your oldest group of students served during 2004-05 (i.e., your grant project closeout year) were in 11th grade or younger, please answer the following questions. (a) What is oldest grade level served in your "closeout year"? (b) How many students were in that grade level? (This number should equal the number of students in the oldest grade level for which data were provided on Row 1 on the above table.) (c) What year are these students scheduled to graduate from high school?

Also note: If the oldest students in your closeout year are in 11th grade or younger, do not respond to Question 3 – Question 5.

3) **"High School Completion/Graduation rates" for the Class of 2005:** What is the number of the 12th graders during 2004-05 ("Class of 2005") who received an official high school diploma from any of your GEAR UP high schools?

4) **"Immediate postsecondary education institution enrollment rates" for Class of 2005:** What is the number of cohort students from the Class of 2005 who enrolled by the fall immediately following receipt of high school diploma in a: (a) less than 2-year postsecondary education institution, (b) 2–3 year postsecondary education institution, and (c) 4 or more year postsecondary education institution?

Figure 9–2 *continues*

SECTION VI: GRANT BUDGET INFORMATION

Please complete the Financial Status Report (SF 269), according to its attached instructions, and the 6-year Federal Expenditures and Matching Contributions table below.

In the following table, please provide information about your Federal and matching expenditures for *previous, completed budget periods*. For example, since your grant began in Fiscal Year 1999, the Year 1 budget period would be September 1999 through August 2000. Fill out information for ALL completed budget periods, Years 1–6.

	Actual Federal Expenditures Year 1	Actual Matching Contributions Year 1	Actual Federal Expenditures Year 2	Actual Matching Contributions Year 2	Actual Federal Expenditures Year 3	Actual Matching Contributions Year 3	Actual Federal Expenditures Year 4	Actual Matching Contributions Year 4	Actual Federal Expenditures Year 5	Actual Matching Contributions Year 5	Actual Federal Expenditures Year 6	Actual Matching Contributions Year 6
1. Salaries and Wages												
2. Employee Benefits												
3. Travel												
4. Equipment Purpose												
5. Materials & Supplies												
6. Consultants & Contracts												
7. Other												
A. Total Direct Costs: (Add lines 1–7)												
B. Total Indirect Costs												
C. Scholarships/Tuition Assistance												
D. TOTAL COSTS (A+B+C)												

If you did not expend Federal and/or matching funds as originally budgeted, please provide an explanation for the change(s) that occurred. Discuss any relevant documents received by the U.S. Department of Education that allowed such change(s).

Figure 9–2 *continued*

Workforce Housing Reward Grant Program

Final Grant Report and Closeout Certification

Contractor: _____ Contract No.: _____

Address: _____

Contact Name: _____ Title: _____

E-mail: _____ Phone: _____

Contract Dollar Amount: $ _____

A. Capital Asset Acquisitions and Project Descriptions

    1. For _all_ capital assets acquired or rehabilitated in whole or in part with WFH funds, please include the project name as detailed in the Scope of Work (Exhibit A) of the Standard Agreement, a description of the capital asset acquired or rehabilitated and the total amount WFH funds used (attach additional sheets if necessary).

Project Name	Capital Asset	Total Cost	WFH Funds Expended Relative to Total Cost	Category

WFH Final Report and Closeout Certification
Revised July 2007

Figure 9–3 *Closeout report requirements.*

Source: Workforce Housing Reward Grant Program, California Department of Housing and Community Development.

2. Please attach, on a separate sheet, a complete narrative for each project funded in whole or in part with WFH funds. The narrative must include, at a minimum, the following information for each project outlined in Section A1:
   - A description of the project
   - The community benefit provided by the project

B. Certifications (Pursuant to Health & Safety Code Section 50544):

Total number of residential units permitted during the calendar year (as provided in WFH application):		Total number of residential units permitted that have resulted in a Certificate of Occupancy or Notice of Completion:	
Very Low-Income	Low-Income	Very Low-Income	Low-Income

C. Closeout Certification:

I hereby certify that all activities undertaken by the _____ (name of Grantee) with funds provided under the WFH Program Standard Agreement have, to the best of my knowledge, been carried out in accordance with the agreement; that proper provision has been made by the Grantee for the payment of all costs and claims; that the State of California is under no obligation to make further payment to the Grantee under the grant agreement; and that every statement and amounts set forth in the Final Grant Cash Request and this Final Grant Closeout Report are, to the best of my knowledge, true and correct. In addition, City/County agrees to retain all records which disclose the activities funded by the Grant including adequate documentation of each transaction for a period of 3 years after the final payment under the Standard Agreement.

Name of Authorized Representative _____

Title of Authorized Representative _____

Signature _____   **Date** _____

> [Print & Mail to HCD]

For HCD Use Only	
Program Representative_____	Approval Date _____
Program Manager _____	Approval Date _____

Report Submittal

Grantees may email the report directly to the Department by clicking the "Submit by Email" button above or by printing and mailing to the address below:

Department of Housing & Community Development
Attn: WFH Program Staff
1800 Third Street, Room 430
Sacramento, CA 95811

WFH Final Report and Closeout Certification
Page 2 of 3

Figure 9–3 *continued*

Required Final Programmatic Reports

Grantees should read the terms and conditions to find out the specific information that should be included in the final programmatic report. Usually, this report includes a description of program accomplishments during the funding period and the benefits from carrying out the project. Funders may also ask for a description of the challenges that arose during the project and how those challenges were resolved. If they were not resolved, grantees may be asked to give an explanation of why not.

Figure 9–4 shows a sample final project report from a grantee who received funds from the Technology Opportunities Program of the U.S. Department of Commerce. The Technology Opportunities Program supported demonstrations of new telecommunications and information technologies to provide education, health care, and public information in the public and nonprofit sectors. **Figure 9–5** shows a form that meets the final reporting requirements for the Value-Added Producer Grant Program of the U.S. Department of Agriculture. Grants may be used for planning activities and for working capital for marketing value-added agricultural products and for farm-based renewable energy. The final reporting requirements for grantees of the Robert Wood Johnson Foundation can be found in **Figure 9–6**. The foundation focuses on the pressing health and health-care issues facing the United States.

Required Final Financial Report

Most funders will require a grantee to submit a final financial report that accounts for all expenditures of grant funds. Expenditures are separated into budget line items, and the total spent should equal the total amount of the grant award. Funders deal with unspent grant funds in a few ways, such as requiring the funds to be returned or allowing the grantee to make additional purchases related to the project.

Keep in mind that if the total amount of the grant award is not spent, it will be hard to convince a funder that funds are need for a continuation of the project. It is a better grants management practice to monitor expenditures carefully, and if allowable, submit a budget revision to the funder requesting that funds be used for other costs related to the project. (See **Figure 9–7**, the Sample Prior Approval form from the National Endowment for the Humanities.)

If a funder required matching funds as a condition of awarding the grant, grantees may also be asked to submit a document that verifies that all matching funds were received. This document should also include the source of the matching funds and if in-kind contributions were received, the dollar value of those contributions. A sample in-kind contribution report from the National Endowment for the Arts is found in **Figure 9–8**.

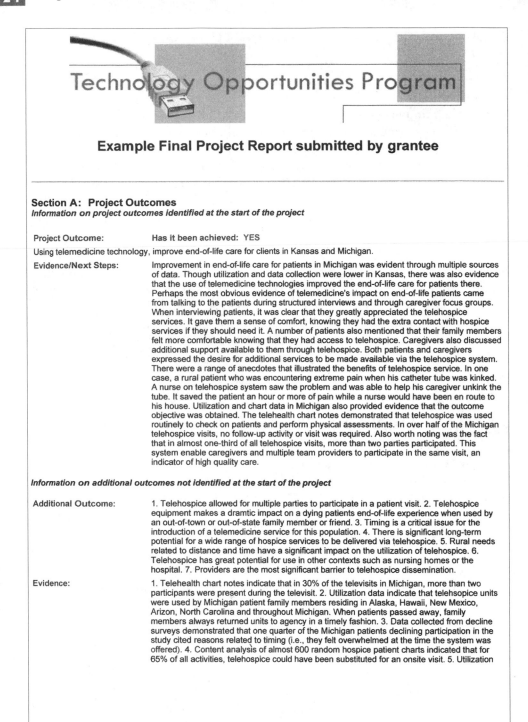

Technology Opportunities Program

Example Final Project Report submitted by grantee

Section A: Project Outcomes
Information on project outcomes identified at the start of the project

Project Outcome:　　　　　Has it been achieved: YES

Using telemedicine technology, improve end-of-life care for clients in Kansas and Michigan.

Evidence/Next Steps:　　　Improvement in end-of-life care for patients in Michigan was evident through multiple sources of data. Though utilization and data collection were lower in Kansas, there was also evidence that the use of telemedicine technologies improved the end-of-life care for patients there. Perhaps the most obvious evidence of telemedicine's impact on end-of-life patients came from talking to the patients during structured interviews and through caregiver focus groups. When interviewing patients, it was clear that they greatly appreciated the telehospice services. It gave them a sense of comfort, knowing they had the extra contact with hospice services if they should need it. A number of patients also mentioned that their family members felt more comfortable knowing that they had access to telehospice. Caregivers also discussed additional support available to them through telehospice. Both patients and caregivers expressed the desire for additional services to be made available via the telehospice system. There were a range of anecdotes that illustrated the benefits of telehospice service. In one case, a rural patient who was encountering extreme pain when his catheter tube was kinked. A nurse on telehospice system saw the problem and was able to help his caregiver unkink the tube. It saved the patient an hour or more of pain while a nurse would have been en route to his house. Utilization and chart data in Michigan also provided evidence that the outcome objective was obtained. The telehealth chart notes demonstrated that telehospice was used routinely to check on patients and perform physical assessments. In over half of the Michigan telehospice visits, no follow-up activity or visit was required. Also worth noting was the fact that in almost one-third of all telehospice visits, more than two parties participated. This system enable caregivers and multiple team providers to participate in the same visit, an indicator of high quality care.

Information on additional outcomes not identified at the start of the project

Additional Outcome:　　　1. Telehospice allowed for multiple parties to participate in a patient visit. 2. Telehospice equipment makes a dramtic impact on a dying patients end-of-life experience when used by an out-of-town or out-of-state family member or friend. 3. Timing is a critical issue for the introduction of a telemedicine service for this population. 4. There is significant long-term potential for a wide range of hospice services to be delivered via telehospice. 5. Rural needs related to distance and time have a significant impact on the utilization of telehospice. 6. Telehospice has great potential for use in other contexts such as nursing homes or the hospital. 7. Providers are the most significant barrier to telehospice dissemination.

Evidence:　　　　　　　　1. Telehealth chart notes indicate that in 30% of the televisits in Michigan, more than two participants were present during the televisit. 2. Utilization data indicate that telehsopice units were used by Michigan patient family members residing in Alaska, Hawaii, New Mexico, Arizon, North Carolina and throughout Michigan. When patients passed away, family members always returned units to agency in a timely fashion. 3. Data collected from decline surveys demonstrated that one quarter of the Michigan patients declining participation in the study cited reasons related to timing (i.e., they felt overwhelmed at the time the system was offered). 4. Content analysis of almost 600 random hospice patient charts indicated that for 65% of all activities, telehospice could have been substituted for an onsite visit. 5. Utilization

Figure 9–4 *Final project report.*
Source: *Technology Opportunities Program, U.S. Department of Commerce.*

data in Michigan indicate that even though there are higher numbers of urban patients enrolled in hospice, only 55% of all telehospice patients resided in urban areas. More importantly, only 45% of all televists were conducted with urban patients and 55% were conducted with the rural patients. 6. This project design excluded patients not living at home. Yet, in Michigan, more than 70% of decline forms were initiated by nurses because the patient did not meet study design criteria such as living at home. 7. Data from pre- and post-provider surveys in Michigan indicated that providers have a pre-conceived notion regarding telehospice that does significantly change over time. Providers who embrace this solution early on account for almost all utilization.

Section B: Project Accomplishments
The accomplishments of the project

The project's most significant accomplishment or achievement

The project's most significant accomplishment was proving the efficacy of telehospice use in the field. It was evident that patients both enjoy the telehospice calls and feel an increased sense of comfort at having telehospice services at their disposal. Potential cost savings were also evident, as there were instances where a problem was solved via the telehospice service that would have traditionally required a nurse to drive to patients' homes. This saved the hospice providers both the cost of the nurses' time in driving to patients' homes, and savings in gas money. As mentioned above, there were problems solved via telehospice that traditionally would have required a nurse to visit a patient's home. This has the benefit of improving patient care, showing that telehospice works in real world settings.

Changes in the way in which end-users performed their jobs or carried out their activities

The work functions of providers who embraced telehospice changed considerably with the introduction of telehospice services. Active telehsopice users supplemented and replaced onsite vists with patients. Some performed a televisit prior to an onsite visit to determine any special equipment or supplies that might be worth bringing to the traditional visit. A variety of examples emerged that demonstrate how telehsopice providers incorporated the system into their delivery strategies. In one case, the caregiver of a patient in an urban setting called Hospice of Michigan extremely anxious because her husband was bleeding from the neck, and she did not know what to do. A nurse instructed her to get the telehospice unit, and that nurse instructed the caregiver about what she should be doing while another nurse was en route to the patient's home. The caregiver's anxiety level decreased upon seeing the nurse's face, and the caregiver was on the phone waiting for the nurse to arrive at their home. Additionally, the nurses involved were able to communicate findings with one another via the telehospice units. Telehospice presented a new opportunity for teamwork among providers - one provider talking to the patient via telehospice while another was en route to the patient's home to solve a problem in person. In one case, a nurse received a call from her patient that was complaining of upper chest, neck, and arm pain. The patient had a cardiac history and could have been having spinal cord compression due to his terminal illness. The nurse got on the telehospice unit while another nurse was sent to his home. Using the telehospice equipment, the nurse could see the patient and that he was not appropriately following her instructions to relieve his pain. She then instructed him on what he was doing wrong, and how he could correctly work to relieve his pain. She stayed on the telehospice call with the patient until a nurse arrived at the patient's home, and the two nurses used the telehospice units to consult about the patient's care.

The impact of the project on the community at large

The telehospice project had a significant impact on the community; particularly rural communities where the entire area was familiar with the service and its advantages. Below are two anecdotes that illustrate some of the ways telehospice was used to make a difference in the lives of those who took part in the project. "Perhaps the most touching story of the telehospice project was when a unit was installed in a nursing home for a forty-year-old patient who had a five-year-old daughter that lived seventy-five miles away. The patient was only able to see her daughter every two weeks, until a telehospice unit was installed in her daughter's home. The day the patient was being instructed how to use the unit happened to be the daughter's sixth birthday, and her daughter brought all her presents to the camera and was able to share the day with her mother. The patient was crying, saying, 'You have no idea what you've given me. For me to be able to see my daughter every day is something no words could ever express.' For two weeks the patient was able to see her daughter at least every day through telehospice, helping her with homework and sharing stories. The patient improved emotionally in her final weeks as she was satisfied and fulfilled. She died two weeks later. Telehospice presented a unique opportunity to provide this patient with true quality end of life care." "A golfer on the PGA Senior Tour, Allen Doyle, was touring a Hospice of Michigan building in Detroit. A telehospice patient near Alpena lived in a golf course community and had been an avid golfer his entire life, before his illness prevented him from playing. Allen made a telehospice call to this patient, and it meant the world for the patient to talk with Doyle face to face using the telehospice equipment. The patient talked about that call many times before his death." Telehospice has also been used to connect patients and caregivers to distant family located around the country, including Alaska, Hawaii, Florida, New Mexico, Arizona, and North Carolina. This is another way telehospice has worked to improve the lives of those involved with the project. Finally, telehospice improved the care of rural patients who traditionally had to wait longer periods of time for a provider could reach their house. With telehospice these rural patients can receive

Figure 9–4 *continues*

care immediately, a great improvement in the care of a traditionally underserved population.

A description of unanticipated problems that resulted from the project

The most significant unanticipated problem related to the telehospice project may have been the difficulty in getting the providers themselves to buy into the program. The project simply never really got off the ground at some sites in Kansas, due mainly to a lack of buy-in from the providers and/or their managers. In Michigan, project planners never successfully acieved deployment in the Extended Coverage group at Hospice of Michigan. The people in charge of Extended Coverage chose not to make use of telehospice in many cases, despite the efforts of the research team to encourage its use a benficial tool for the Extended Coverage team. There were instances when telehospice could have improved the care of patients who called in to Extended Coverage after hours care, but it was not frequently used. This lack of provider support was due to both turnover in the management of Extended Coverage and a general lack of interest from the management of Extended Coverage. Overall, the challenge of universal provider buy-in was the real unanticipated problem, as getting the patients to support and use telehospice services was relatively straightforward. Some providers immediately saw the advantages of telehospice and used frequently. Many others did not want to be bothered with what they perceived to extra work.

The number of individuals who have benefitted (directly and indirectly) from TOP-related equipment or resources since the beginning of the project

	End Users	Other Beneficiaries
Number in human service settings	0	0
Number in cultural settings	0	0
Number in government agencies	0	0
Number in public safety settings	0	0
Number in educational settings	0	0
Number in health care settings	325	150
Other end users/other (specify): Family members located in distant states	15	0
Total number of direct and indirect beneficiaries	340	150

Section C: Project Expansion
Information on the expansion of the project

Has the project expanded to serve additional end users in locations or organizations beyond those targeted in the TOP proposal: Yes

A description of the (1) scope of the expansion; (2) the number/characteristics of additional end users being served; (3) the funding sources for their expansion; and (4) the approximate dollar amount or value of any additional equipment or resources that were leveraged by your project as part of the expansion.

Hospice of Michigan has obtained an additional $60,000 (from an SBC Foundation grant and private donations)to purchase more equipment for service expansion. All of these funds were obtained due to success from TIIAP telehospice project.

Section D: Spin-Off Activities
Information on spin-off activities from the project

Has the TOP project generated any spin-off activities? Yes

A description of any spin-off activities and the additional services that are being provided.

A statewide proposal has been submitted to expand telehsopice across the entire state of Michigan. Word on funding is still pending.

Figure 9–4 *continued*

Section E: Partnerships
Information on project partners

Describe how your project partnership worked?

The partnership between Michigan State University and Hospice of Michigan was extremely successful. Both organizations displayed significant dedication and devotion to the project and a high level of mutual trust was established early in the project. Open and frequent communication was a key strategy. Project personnel from MSU and HOM met every Monday without excpetion at 2:00 to go over key issues. In addition, the project coordinator at HOM was required to send a weekly email to all telehsopice offices in Michigan reporting on their level of activity that week and significant events. Periodic visits were made to all telehospice sites and periodic project updates were provided to staff at all participating offices. Personnel from MSU and HOM jointly presented study findings to conferences and local meetings and are currently collaborating on joint publications. Both MSU and HOM are actively looking for opportunities for future collaboration regarding telehospice research. MSU participants provide ongoing support as HOM obtains donations for future telehospice service expansion. HOM should be considered one of the premier telehospice providers in the nation. The relationship between KU Medical Center and its partners did not prove to be as fruitful. After making a commitment to participate in the project, the urban arm of Hospice Inc. and Kansas City Hospice both pulled out of the project.

Section F: Lessons Learned
Information on the lessons learned from the project

The most significant barrier or obstacle that the project had to overcome

Hospice providers make or break the successful use of telehospice. Nurses, social workers, and other providers are the primary gatekeepers to the use of telehospice services for patients. We know that patients are comfortable receiving services via telehospice, yet this can only happen if their provider will use this innovation. Pre and post survey data informed us that experience does not have the impact we had hoped to see. Providers have pre-conceived notions about whether they want to use this technology or not, and watching others successfully employ this technology does not appear to sway those with little enthusiasm for telehospice. This has significant implications for how hospice organizations should launch and employ telehospice services in the future.

A description of any lessons that the project has learned that would be of use to future TOP projects

Strongly consider timing and endusers. Telehospice was adopted more readily and demonstrated a more significant contribution for rural patients as compared to urban patients. Providers in rural hospice offices in both states identified applications and benefits more readily than their urban counterparts. Even though there are delivery challenges in urban areas, the sheer distance to reach rural patients dominates as the most important benefit of telehospice. Also, it is important to carefully time when a patient is offered telehospice. A great number of patient refusals for telehospice are directly attributable to feelings of being overwhelmed when patient is first being enrolled into hospice care. This is an extremely sensitive event, often when patients and caregivers are accepting the inevitability of death. Many patients are better prepared to consider telehospice a week or two into their hospice enrollment.

A recommendation that future projects replicate/adapt the TOP-related approach used by your project (YES/NO)

Yes

A description of any lessons or advice that your would pass on to projects that are replicating/adapting this approach

The academic/private organization approach was extremely important, particularly in Michigan. MSU researchers designed and evaluated the project. However, the project was carried out in an unrelated organization. The objectivity brought to the evaluation of this endeavor proved to be crucial. MSU was able to be candid and honest in its assessment of what really worked and what didn't. Most importantly, MSU was unable to inappropriately influence, adjust, or frame results from this project. This is an important element missing from many telemedicine projects that implement and evaluate within the same organization. Both MSU and HOM greatly benefitted from the university/private organization partnership.

Section G: Impact of the TOP Grant
Impact of the grant on the organization and community(s) served

The most likely outcome of the project if it did not received Federal funds through the TOP program

The activity would probably never been implemented.

How the absence of TOP funding would have affected the range of services offered by the project

How the absence of TOP funding would have affected the scale of the project

Figure 9–4 *continues*

How the absence of TOP funding would have affected the implementation schedule of your project

Specific examples of how the support provided through the TOP program impacted the scope, scale, and success of your project

> The funding through the TOP program made it possible to purchase the actual equipment used to provide telehospice services in Michigan and Kansas. Most importantly, however, was that TOP funding enabled objective personnel to evaluate the project. These evaluation personnel, housed at universities, have a self interest in disseminating the results of the project. Thus papers and conference presentations will occur for several years post project completion. While it is possible other funding could have been found, it is unlikely that the project would have been able to support nearly so many patients or allow for data collection and dissemination.

Section H: Future Plans
Information on future plans for project

The current status of the project

> In full operation.

> **Factors**

> Mechanical obsolescence (equipment became inoperable, unreliable, worn out)

> Technological obsolescence (faster, more accurate, better alternatives became available)

> Personnel changes (project staff who were most interested are no longer involved)

> Insufficient funding available for maintenance of project-related activities

> Loss of partners or failure of partnerships

> Lack of community support

> Too costly to maintain/sustain

> Policy barriers (specify): *False*

The future plans are envisioned for the project

> In Kansas, telehospice services will continue in the rural communities that participated in the project. No activity is planned for the prior urban paritipants. In Michigan, Hospice of Michigan has obtained $60,000 in funding to expand the service within its own agency. These funds came from SBC Foundation funding and private donations. Michigan State University, in parntership with Hospice of Michigan, Hospice of SW Michigan, and a hospice agency located in Michigan's Upper Peninsula, has submitted a proposal to launch telehospice across the entire state of Michigan. Funding notification is still pending.

Section I: Other
Additional topics or areas not previously addressed

> This project has been exceptionally well received, particularly in Michigan. Perhaps the most telling evidence of a telemedicine project is its sustainability post grant funding. Telehospice is an integral service within HOM and will continue through internal funding and support. Perhaps one question missing from this closeout survey concerns new areas of service or reseacrh that became evident from this project. In our case, it has become evident that telehospice needs to be explored as an option for hospice caregivers, in addition to hospice patients. In Michigan, project participants have become policy activitis in search of strategies to widen services for hospice caregivers. In an ideal world, it would be nice to see a mechanism between NTIA and other federal agencies such as NIH so that ideas could be forwarded regarding important outcomes-based research that should follow TOP projects.

Figure 9–4 *continued*

Committed to the future
of rural communities.

**Business and
Cooperative
Programs**

 Go

Value-Added Producer Grant
Post-Award Reporting Requirements

You must provide Rural Development with a hard copy original or an electronic copy that includes all required signatures of the following reports. The reports should be submitted to the Agency contact listed for your assigned state. Failure to submit satisfactory reports on time may result in suspension or termination of your grant. RBS is currently developing an online reporting system. Once the system is developed, you may be required to submit some or all of your reports online instead of in hard copy.

1. Form SF-269 or SF-269A. A "Financial Status Report," listing expenditures according to agreed upon budget categories, on a semi-annual basis. Reporting periods end each March 31 and September 30. Reports are due 30 days after the reporting period ends.

2. Semi-annual performance reports that compare accomplishments to the objectives stated in the proposal. Identify all tasks completed to date and provide documentation supporting the reported results. If the original schedule provided in the work plan is not being met, the report should discuss the problems or delays that may affect completion of the project. Objectives for the next reporting period should be listed. Compliance with any special condition on the use of award funds should be discussed. Reports are due as provided in paragraph (1) of this section. The supporting documentation for completed tasks include, but are not limited to, feasibility studies, marketing plans, business plans, articles of incorporation and bylaws and an accounting of how working capital funds were spent. Planning grant projects must also report the estimated increase in revenue, increase in customer base, number of jobs created, and any other relevant economic indicators generated by continuing the project into its operational phase. Working capital grants must report the increase in revenue, increase in customer base, number of jobs created, and any other relevant economic indicators generated

Figure 9–5 *Final reporting requirements.*

Source: Value-Added Producer Grant Program, U.S. Department of Agriculture.

by the project during the grant period. Projects with significant energy components must also report expected or actual capacity (e.g. gallons of ethanol produced annually, megawatt hours produced annually) and any emissions reductions incurred during the project.

3. Final project performance reports, inclusive of supporting documentation. The final performance report is due within 90 days of the completion of the project.

Figure 9–5 *continued*

Grantee Reporting Instructions

Final Narrative Report

Robert Wood Johnson Foundation

FINAL NARRATIVE REPORT—OVERVIEW AND PURPOSE

- The Final Narrative Report is filed at the end of your grant before it can close. If you have had a multiyear grant, it replaces the Annual Narrative Report for the last year. Include all the activities and accomplishments of the entire grant, including the final year in your Final Narrative Report.

- The Final Narrative Report asks seven questions that are designed to elicit essential information about the results, findings and lessons from your project, and how well it met its stated goals or objectives.

- Support your answers with quantitative data, where they are available and appropriate; provide other supportive evidence where requested.

- Use "None" and "Not applicable" where appropriate.

FORMAT

- The maximum length of a Final Narrative Report is 10 pages, including any charts and tables. The preferred length is five to seven pages.

- Use a 12-point font, one-inch margins and single-line spacing.

- Incorporate the seven questions as bold italic subheads.

- Do not include appendixes, attachments or exhibits in your report.

- The Final Bibliography is a separate report.

COVER PAGE

- Prepare the cover page of the report on a sheet of your institution's or organization's letterhead.

- Include address, telephone number and e-mail address, if these are not printed on your stationery.

- Date the page.

- Head it FINAL NARRATIVE REPORT followed by:

  - the title of the project;

  - for projects within national programs, the name of the program;

  - the five-digit RWJF grant identification number;

  - the dates covered by the entire grant. If the project has been granted a no-cost extension, indicate the time period of the extension in parentheses;

  - the total amount of the grant; and

  - the goal of the project as described in the proposal.

(continues)

Figure 9–6 *Grantee reporting instructions.*

Grantee Reporting Instructions

Final Narrative Report

Robert Wood Johnson Foundation

BIBLIOGRAPHY

The Final Bibliography submitted with your Final Narrative Report is a comprehensive catalog of the products (e.g., books, journal articles, reports, brochures, Web sites), national/regional events (e.g., conferences and workshops), and published presentations and testimony your project produced. If you produced any products, a Final Bibliography must be provided with the Final Narrative Report.

SUBMITTING REPORTS, BIBLIOGRAPHIES AND PRODUCTS

Within 30 days of the end of your grant period please submit to your *grants administrator*:

- **two copies** of the Final Narrative Report and **two copies** of the Final Bibliography, clipped together;

- **two copies** of those materials (grant products) that have been produced in the current reporting period. For multiyear grants, include only those materials not submitted previously. Each set of products must be accompanied by an additional copy of the Final Bibliography.

Your *grants administrator* will distribute your Final Narrative Report and Final Bibliography within RWJF.

If you are a grantee within a national program with a national program office, also submit one copy of your Final Narrative Report, your Final Bibliography and your grant products to the national program office.

FINAL NARRATIVE REPORT—QUESTIONS

1. **What measurable goals did you set for this project and what indicators did you use to measure your performance? To what extent has your project achieved these goals and levels of performance?** Briefly describe what the project actually did to meet its goals. If the goals of the project have not been met, explain what happened and why. If there were additional accomplishments, describe them, and explain how and why the activities that led to these accomplishments were undertaken. Be as specific as possible. Cover the areas described below that are applicable to your project:

   - If you conducted a review of literature to help direct your project, describe key findings and how they were used.

   - If you worked in collaboration or cooperation with other organizations or institutions, describe those arrangements and their importance to the project.

   - For a service project, indicate the number of people served in total during the project, and what, where and how services were provided, and over what time period. If services are continuing, indicate the number of people currently being served.

   - For a project making individual awards for training, leadership development or recognition, indicate the kinds of awards provided during the grant and the results of the awards, including any special accomplishments.

   - For a project that aimed to create institutional change, indicate the various activities and methods that have been undertaken to effect such change and their success in doing so.

   - For a communications project, describe the products produced, the number produced, the number disseminated and by what means, to whom, the size of the audience reached, when these activities took place, and the reaction received in the media (reviews and media coverage) and in the public sector. If a Web site was produced, provide the address, the name of the organization or individual that started the site, the date it went live, the number of people visiting it on a monthly basis, the content of the site and how it relates to the grant.

Figure 9–6 *continued*

Grantee Reporting Instructions

Final Narrative Report

Robert Wood Johnson Foundation

- For an evaluation project, describe the evaluation methodology and the major findings from the evaluation.

- For a research project, describe the subject matter of the research, the time period, the universe and the response rate (if applicable). If your research depended on existing data, describe how accessible you found the data; if existing data needed to be integrated with data collected by this grant, describe the ease or difficulty of that integration. Describe the major findings of your research. Use a bulleted format, with one bullet for each key finding.

2. **Did the project encounter internal or external challenges? How were they addressed? Was there something RWJF could have done to assist you?** Describe each challenge and the actions you undertook to address it.

- What was the effect on the project?

- If a change negatively affected the project, how did you attempt to cope with it?

- What could RWJF have done to assist you?

3. **Has your organization received funding from other foundations, corporations or government bodies for the project RWJF has been supporting?**

- If so, please give each funder's name, the amount provided and when it was provided. If you only know the total provided, put that total amount, what funders contributed to it, with any amounts you know for sure that any of these funders provided.

- If the support is in-kind and you can estimate the dollar amount, provide that figure; if it is in-kind and you cannot estimate the amount, do not include it here.

- Did RWJF funding help leverage this other funding or was it unrelated?

- Did the project receive funding after RWJF's funded ended that allowed your organization to continue the work? Please describe the funding and the project's continuation.

4. **When considering the design and implementation of this project, what lessons did you learn that might help other grantees implement similar work in this field?** Please do not discuss specific findings or results of the project. Instead consider your process of implementing and executing this project, including, for example:

- What steps you took during the planning stages to:

  - involve key stakeholders; and

  - allow for changes in key objectives in response to changes "on the ground."

- What elements of your implementation strategy worked, or did not work, and why?

Figure 9–6 *continues*

Grantee Reporting Instructions

Final Narrative Report

Robert Wood Johnson Foundation

5. **What impact do you think the project has had to date? Who can be contacted a few years from now to follow up on the project?** Describe what you believe to be the impact of the project, providing evidence for all statements (e.g., publication in major journals, citations of the project in literature, major press coverage, adoption of the model by other organizations). For example:

- Has the project contributed in some significant way to general knowledge about a subject? Or to a change in conventional wisdom?

- Has it increased the public's access to information?

- Has it created a new model for delivering services or conducting research?

- Has it informed the work of other professionals or organizations?

- Has it informed the work of other researchers?

- Has it changed an institution so that it is better able to fulfill its mission?

Give us the name and contact information of someone who can be contacted in a few years if RWJF wants to follow up on the impact.

6. **What are the post-grant plans for the project if it does not conclude with the grant?** Include a description of the following that are applicable:

- Changes in operations and scope.

- Replication or use of findings.

- Names of other institutions you expect to involve.

- Plans to support the project financially, including grants you are seeking or have received and/or a business plan to become self-supporting.

- If you obtained matching funds during the grant, has this affected your ability to obtain financial support for the project's continued operation as the grant ends?

- Communications plans.

RWJF has an ongoing interest in the effects and accomplishments of your project over the long run and welcomes updates on the continuation, dissemination or replication of your work after your grant is closed. Please send any such news, marked with the grant identification number, to the Grant Results Reporting Unit in RWJF's Communications Office, which regularly reports on completed grants and will share this information with the *program officer*.

Figure 9–6 *continued*

Grantee Reporting Instructions

Final Narrative Report

Robert Wood Johnson Foundation

7. **With a perspective on the entire project, what have been its key publications and national/regional communications activities? Did the project meet its communications goals?**

- If there have been no communication efforts, say so, and give the reason.

- If there have been national or regional communications activities, describe them here, noting the size of the audience they reached and their significance (e.g., publication in a peer-reviewed journal, speech at a national conference, a press briefing, an unusual and important request for copies of a book or a report). Then describe any plans you may have for the future.

- If your communications activities were local in nature, summarize them here. Such activities include presentations about the project to any number of local organizations or media coverage about the project from an array of local media. For example:

  - "Project staff made 50 presentations about the project across the state of Idaho to organizations such as B'nai B'rith, Area Agencies on Aging and local AARP chapters."

  - "The project received coverage in 12 newspapers in the state, including the *Montclair Times*, the *Verona/Cedar Grove Sentinel* and the *Summit Express*."

- If you have produced any products (e.g., books, journal articles, reports, brochures, Web sites) about the project, conducted conferences or workshops, made presentations that were published in proceedings or gave testimony before a governmental body, you are required to submit a Final Bibliography. The Final Bibliography does not cover all categories of grant products requested by RWJF. (Instructions for Sending Grant Products to RWJF and Submitting a Bibliography, including categories of entries and entry formats are included here.)

If, after the grant is closed, an article, report or book is published, the project receives media coverage, or there are other significant communications activities, please send two copies of each product to the Grant Results Reporting Unit, marked with the grant identification number. For videotapes, audiotapes and all computer disks produced under the grant, please also mark each item with a two-line description of the contents, where it was produced, and where and when it was broadcast or presented.

First review the list of grant products, then use the bibliography formats to write your Final Bibliography.

Figure 9–6 *continued*

SAMPLE PRIOR APPROVAL FORM

NEH Grant Number: _____ Other Identifying #: _____

Project Director: _____

Current Grant Period: From _____ To _____

Requested by:_____ Date of Request: _____
       (if other than project director)

Check the type of change that is being requested and explain why the change(s) is needed in the space provided on the reverse side of this form.

* The grantee institution is authorized to approve the items which are asterisked.

[ ]   EXTEND THE GRANT PERIOD
      Number of months _____
      *( ) 1st extension of 12 months or less
       ( ) 1st extension exceeding 12 months
       ( ) 2nd extension

      A one-time extension of up to 12 months can be made if additional time is required to complete the original scope of the project with funds already made available. At least ten days before the grant is scheduled to expire, the Office of Grant Management must be informed in writing of the new expiration date and the reason the grant had to be extended. A second request or a request to extend the grant for more than twelve months must include a detailed justification for the extension, an estimate of the unexpended funds and a plan of work for activities that will be undertaken during the requested extension period.

[ ]   BUDGET REVISION

      *( )   Transfer of budgeted funds between direct cost categories.
      *( )   Transfer of budgeted funds between direct and indirect costs.
      *( )   Addition of the following costs that were not included in the budget approved by NEH.
          __ foreign travel,
          __ equipment purchase,
          __ stipends and travel allowances for participants at conferences, symposia,
         and training projects,
          __ publication and printing costs.
       ( )   Transfer to a third party of a portion of work under this grant.
       ( )   Addition of costs that are specifically disallowed by the
          terms and conditions of the grant award.
       ( )   Transfer of funds from stipends or training allowances to other budget categories.

[ ]   *INCUR PREAWARD COSTS WITHIN 90 DAYS OF THE BEGINNING DATE OF THE GRANT.

[ ]   CHANGE IN PROJECT ACTIVITIES THAT AFFECT SCOPE

      Written NEH approval is needed before a grantee may make a change in project activities that affects in any way the purpose of the grant, the subject matter, the treatment of the subject matter, the historical time frame of the project, the volume of material that is to be treated/studied, or the products that are expected to result from grant activities. In making such a request, the grantee should understand that NEH's authority to approve changes that affect the scope of a project is limited by its legislation and appropriation law. **(Explain in detail why a change in project activities is necessary and what change is proposed).**

Figure 9–7 *Prior approval form.*
Source: National Endowment for the Humanities.

[ ]   CHANGE IN KEY PROJECT PERSONNEL

The replacement of the project director, the co-director, or other project personnel whose replacement is restricted in the grant award or a substantial reduction in the level of their effort (e.g., their unanticipated absence for more than three months, or a twenty-five percent reduction in the time devoted to the project) requires prior written approval from NEH. (Evidence of the qualifications of replacement personnel must be provided).

[ ]   OTHER CHANGE

Explanation/justification of requested changes. (Use attachment if additional space is needed).

_____

REQUESTED CHANGES
      ( ) APPROVED   ( ) NOT APPROVED

_____ _____ _____
      (signature)   (title)   (date)

DOES NEH HAVE TO APPROVE REQUEST OR BE NOTIFIED OF CHANGE? ( ) YES ( ) NO
IF YES, DATE SENT _____

Figure 9–7 *continued*

SAMPLE IN-KIND CONTRIBUTION REPORT

Report of
SERVICES RENDERED, GOODS DONATED, FACILITIES PROVIDED
to the

_____
(Name of Organization)

Project: _____
Donor Organization: _____
       Address: _____
                _____
Donor's Signature: _____ Phone: _____
       Position: _____

Date(s) services were performed, goods were donated, or facilities provided for project:
_____
_____

Services Rendered: VALUE

    by_____ hours _____ $ _____
    by_____ hours _____   _____
    by_____ hours _____   _____
    by_____ hours _____   _____
    by_____ hours _____   _____
    Others listed on reverse; amount from reverse:
                                    Total Services $ _____

Goods Donated:
    Item _____ $ _____
    Item _____   _____
    Item _____   _____
    Others listed on reverse; amount from reverse:
                                    Total Goods $ _____

Facilities Provided:
    Place _____ $ _____
    Place _____   _____
    Place _____   _____
    Place _____   _____
    Others listed on reverse; amount from reverse:
                                    Total Facilities $ _____
                                    TOTAL VALUE $ _____
APPROVED BY:
                    Name: _____
                    Title: _____
                    Date: _____

Note: Please attach an explanation of the bases for the valuation of each item and any supporting documentation.

Figure 9–8 *In-kind contribution report.*
Source: National Endowment for the Arts.

Equipment Inventory

Some grantors allow grantees to purchase equipment with grant funds and may request an equipment inventory at the end of the project. Usually, equipment is not returned after a project is completed. Grantees may be asked to use the equipment only for the same purposes outlined in the original proposal. If the information is not included in the terms and conditions, grantees should check with a program officer to find out if there are any restrictions on equipment use after the project is completed.

Compliance Certification

As a condition of receiving funding, some federal grantors require that grantees comply with specific requirements by the end of the project. For example, the U.S. Department of Homeland security has two compliance requirements of recipients of the Assistance to Firefighters grant funds.

In their final report, grantees must certify compliance with the National Incident Management System and Command System requirements, which relate to management of a major incident (emergency situation) when help is needed from other jurisdictions, the state, and the federal government. Grantees who are fire departments must certify compliance with the National Fire Incident Reporting System requirements for reporting fires and other incidents in a uniform manner. The information about AFG compliance certification is included in the program guidance (request for proposal) document.

Penalties for Not Submitting

As a part of accepting a grant award, a grantee is agreeing to submit all of the forms required by the funder within the time frame that is included in the terms and conditions. If a grantee does not submit the required forms, there can be several consequences. Some funders will not make the final payment of the grant award until the report is received. Some will not allow a grantee to apply for any future funding for any project. Others will not allow a grantee to apply again for a specific time period. The National Endowment for the Arts, for example, states that a grantee is ineligible to receive funding for 5 years if it has not submitted the final report.

Chapter Summary

Grant closeout is a critical piece of the grants management process. Grantees should review the terms and conditions of a grant and make a note of the types of final reports that are due and the deadlines for them. Examples of closeout forms include a programmatic report, a financial report, and, if applicable, a matching funds report and equipment inventory form.

Grantees can suffer serious consequences if the grant is not closed out in the appropriate manner. Typically, the consequences are related to final payments of grant funds and jeopardizing possible future funding from grantors.

Chapter 10

Ethical Issues

Unfortunately, grants management can present a variety of opportunities for unethical behavior to occur. In his book *Ethical Issues in Grantmaking and Grantseeking*, author Michael Josephson cites fundamental ethical issues of the grantmaker–grantseeker relationship. He believes that two of these, honesty and integrity, are critical components of this relationship.

The Issue of Honesty

For grants to be managed effectively and ethically, grantors and grantees should always strive to be honest in their dealings with each other. Neither party should withhold relevant information nor should they mislead one another. In simple terms, in regard to grants management, grantors should make their expectations of grantees clear at the beginning of the grantsmanship process, before an applicant agrees to accept a grant award. This includes specifying all of the terms and conditions of accepting the award in clear language so that applicants can decide if they want to become a grantee.

Grantees should be honest when completing a grant proposal, creating objectives that are realistic and attainable, and developing a budget based on concrete real numbers, rather than on speculation.

Grantees should report all project results, both positive and negative, and should not change the information in programmatic and evaluation reports in order to make the project look more successful. Grantees should keep documentation of all expenditures and be sure that grant funds are only spent on allowable budget items.

The Issue of Integrity

This issue is closely tied to the mission of both the grantor and the grantee. Grantors should exercise caution when making funding decisions and choose proposals describing projects that are closely aligned with the mission. They should also resist coercing or forcing grantees to give up their own mission in order to receive a grant award.

Grantseekers must refrain from mission creep. In other words, they should remain true to their own mission by only approaching funders whose interests are a close match with their mission, rather than promising to provide services that are outside the domain of their organization. Applicants should be willing to turn down a grant award offer if it will require their organization to stray from its mission.

Examples of Mismanagement

The public is probably most familiar with the mismanagement of grant funds because these cases often receive publicity. There are three common mismanagement activities associated with grant funds: (1) using grant monies to purchase items or to pay for services/activities that are not allowable expense items (also called the misapplication of funds); (2) using grant funds for expenses that are totally unrelated to the project that was submitted in the proposal; and (3) commingling grant funds.

Commingling refers to the practice of placing grant funds into an account with funds from other sources. Some grant programs require that grant funds be placed into a separate account so it is possible to document that they were used for grant-related activities and expenditures. **Figure 10–1** shows the findings and recommendations from an Office of the Inspector General (OIG) final inspection report. This OIG report discusses the District of Columbia Housing Authority's commingling of funds from the HOPE VI grant program. The purpose of this Housing and Urban Development program is to redevelop failed housing projects into mixed-income communities. It appears that the District of Columbia Housing Authority placed grant funds into an account that contained several other funding streams. Consequently, it was impossible to document the expenditures for the HOPE VI funds.

In addition to mishandling grant funds, there are several other types of mismanagement to avoid. These include:

- Inflating budget numbers in the proposal
- Having unsupported costs and purchases paid with grant funds

OIG No. 01-2-25PH(c)
Final Report

FINDINGS AND RECOMMENDATIONS

**FINDING 1: ACCOUNTING FOR HOPE VI AND OTHER GRANT/
PRIVATE FUNDING**

SYNOPSIS

Our analysis of DCHA's monthly bank statements for the HOPE VI Program revealed that DCHA did not maintain HOPE VI grant funds in a separate bank account as required by the HOPE VI grant agreements. Instead, HOPE VI funds were deposited and commingled with other types of funds into one bank account, and then re-deposited and disbursed from another bank account. Further, DCHA did not establish a system of recordkeeping that would separately account for expenditures made for each HOPE VI project, and did not maintain a monthly summary or schedule to show the amount of funds disbursed on HOPE VI Program activities. The lack of an effective recordkeeping system, coupled with the commingling of funds, resulted in our inability to identify HOPE VI grant fund disbursements with specific HOPE VI program costs.

These conditions occurred because DCHA did not fully comply with all of the provisions of the HOPE VI grant agreements and the federal regulations for the maintenance and accounting of HOPE VI grant funds. In general, DCHA's senior officials did not ensure that established criteria for tracking program costs were followed. As a result, those responsible for oversight of the HOPE VI grant fund cannot be assured that grant funds were used for HOPE VI activities or disbursed for valid, reimbursable program costs.

DISCUSSION

DCHA neither fully complied with provisions of the HOPE VI grant agreements nor with federal regulations regarding the maintenance and accounting of HOPE VI grant funds. These matters are discussed in more detail below.

Commingling of HOPE VI Grant Funds. The HOPE VI grant agreements prohibit the commingling of grant funds with funds from any other source. For example, Article IV of the HOPE VI Grant agreement for the Wheeler Creek HOPE VI Revitalization Project (Covenant and Conditions) provides, in part:

> In its accounts and recordkeeping, the Grantee will not commingle
> HOPE VI Grant funds with funds from any other Federal, state or
> local government agencies. (Such other funds may be used to carry
> out the Revitalization plan, so long as they are not commingled in the
> Grantee's accounts and record keeping.) The Grantee will ensure that
> HOPE VI grant funds are not used to duplicate work which is funded
> under any other Federal program, or from any other source of funding

(continues)

Figure 10–1 *Findings and recommendations from the Office of Inspector General report of the District of Columbia Housing Authority.*
Source: *Office of Inspector General, District of Columbia.*

OIG No. 01-2-25PH(c)
Final Report

FINDINGS AND RECOMMENDATIONS

under the Revitalization Plan, and will establish controls to assure non-duplication of funding.

Analysis of Bank Statements. In order to gain an understanding of DCHA's disbursement cycle for HOPE VI funds, we analyzed bank statements maintained by DCHA for the General Depository Operating Account (GDOA) for the months ending July 31, 2001, and August 31, 2001, covering a period of July 1, 2001, through August 31, 2001. The analysis showed that deposits in the GDOA for the month of July 2001 came from seven different sources (of which one source of funds was HOPE VI funds), and that deposits in the GDOA for the month of August 2001 came from six different sources (which also included HOPE VI funds).

Based upon our analysis and discussions with DCHA officials, we determined that HOPE VI funds had been commingled with other funds. Using the July 2001 bank statement, the illustration below shows funds from seven different sources that were deposited and commingled into the GDOA.

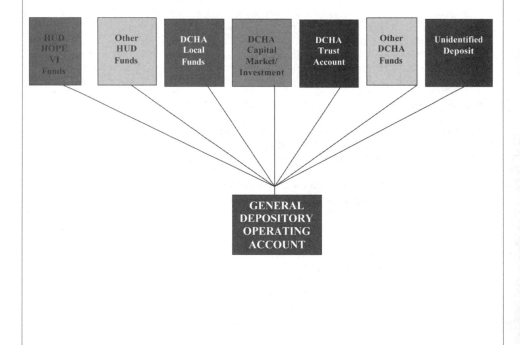

Figure 10–1 *continued*

OIG No. 01-2-25PH(c)
Final Report

FINDINGS AND RECOMMENDATIONS

We discussed the commingling of HOPE VI grant funds with officials of DCHA's Office of Finance. The officials disagreed with our assessment of the grant provision pertaining to the commingling of grant funds, and informed us that Article X of the grant agreement requires that financial records – rather than bank accounts – of programs be maintained separately.

While we agree that financial records of programs are required to be separately maintained, the provisions of the grant agreements clearly require HOPE VI grant funds to be maintained separately from other types of funds. We discussed this with a responsible HUD representative, who agreed that HOPE VI funds should be maintained in a separate bank account. The commingling of HOPE VI funds with other types of funds inhibits accurate accountability, obscures audit trails, and represents a basic breakdown in sound internal controls for the accountability of funds from different funding sources.

Accounting for HOPE VI Funds. The Code of Federal Regulations (CFR) also contains provisions that require funds to be accounted for separately. 24 CFR § 85.20 – Standards for financial management systems states, in part:

> (a) A State must expend and account for grant funds in accordance with State laws and procedures for expending and accounting for its own funds. Fiscal control and accounting procedures of the State, as well as its subgrantees and cost-type contractors, must be sufficient to --
>
> > (1) Permit preparation of reports required by this part and the statutes authorizing the grant, and
> >
> > (2) Permit the tracing of funds to a level of expenditures adequate to establish that such funds have not been used in violation of the restrictions and prohibitions of applicable statutes.

Hope VI Fund Expenditures. Our review of records revealed that DCHA did not establish a system of recordkeeping that would separately account for HOPE VI Program expenditures. Consequently, DCHA could not provide us a monthly summary or schedule to show the amount of funds disbursed for HOPE VI Program activities.

Upon receipt of HOPE VI funds from HUD, the funds pass through two bank accounts: the GDOA (for deposit) and the Public Fund Checking Account (PFCA), from which disbursements to vendors, contactors, developers, and other third parties are made for HOPE VI activities. With the exception of Section 8 Program funds, all program funds that

Figure 10–1 *continues*

OIG No. 01-2-25PH(c)
Final Report

FINDINGS AND RECOMMENDATIONS

DCHA receives are lumped together into the GDOA. DCHA officials explained that funds are transferred from the GDOA to the PFCA on an as needed basis in order to pay bills. The PFCA is the only checking account that DCHA maintains for bill paying purposes. We noted that the total monthly disbursements for HOPE VI Program costs did not agree with the monthly amount deposited. Moreover, we could not identify amounts of HOPE VI funds deposited or the amount of HOPE VI funds disbursed.

DCHA maintains its accounting record of disbursements by vendors rather than by program (such as HOPE VI). However, vendors often supply goods or render services to DCHA for different programs simultaneously. As such, DCHA pays for vendor services with one check, and records the transaction by the total amounts paid to each vendor, with no accompanying breakdown of the amounts that should be charged to each program. For example, a contractor/developer may have been selected to provide services for multiple District projects, such as a specific HOPE VI development project and for other DCHA housing projects (non HOPE VI). When the contractor/developer submits an invoice, the invoice amount is paid for by local DCHA funds. One check is prepared and drawn on the PFCA account to pay for both types of services.

We requested DCHA to prepare a reconciliation report to identify all disbursements for HOPE VI activities for the month of July 2001. In response, DCHA officials stated that no regulation requires DCHA to prepare a monthly reconciliation of HOPE VI funds and, therefore, declined our request. DCHA officials informed us that payments are made to vendors for services rendered for various programs in one check, and because the payments are recorded by vendor, they could not determine which payments are exclusively for the HOPE VI Program.

Finally, DCHA officials explained to us that DCHA uses a Fund Accounting System to maintain its financial records. According to DCHA's rationale, having HOPE VI funds in the same bank account with other types of funds does not result in the commingling of funds. DCHA described the Fund Accounting System as an accounting system used to track specific program costs by using a designated fund number. Working with DCHA personnel on multiple occasions, we tried to track and identify specific HOPE VI income and expenditures by project, but were unsuccessful. Based on these repeated attempts to use the Fund Accounting System to track HOPE VI project income and expenditures, we concluded that DCHA had limited means to account for commingled funds.

CONCLUSION

DCHA deposited and commingled HOPE VI grant funds with other types of funds into one bank account, and did not establish a system of recordkeeping that would separately account for HOPE VI Program expenditures. DCHA did not have a monthly summary or schedule to show the amount of funds disbursed on HOPE VI Program activities. As a result of

Figure 10–1 *continued*

OIG No. 01-2-25PH(c)
Final Report

FINDINGS AND RECOMMENDATIONS

commingling of funds and inadequate recordkeeping, we could not determine whether the HOPE VI grant funds had been properly disbursed for HOPE VI program expenditures.

RECOMMENDATION 1

We recommend that the District of Columbia Housing Authority Director obtain a separate bank account for the maintenance of HOPE VI grant funds for HOPE VI projects.

DCHA Response

DCHA management disagrees with the recommendation, stating that there is no mandatory requirement for establishing separate bank accounts for HOPE VI grant funds. They also contend that this recommendation does not maximize the use of the funds in accordance with good cash management practices.

OIG Comment

DCHA commingled HOPE VI grant funds with other type of funds into one back account, and has not established a system of recordkeeping that separately accounts for HOPE VI program expenditures. The grant agreements provide that HOPE VI funds are not to be commingled with other types of funds in either DCHA's accounts or in its recordkeeping. In order for the funds not to become blended, mixed, or combined, they would have to be maintained separately. When requested, DCHA could not provide a reconciliation report to identify the sources of disbursements for HOPE VI activities. Once disbursed, there was no way to determine what fund sources were being used. We request that DCHA reconsider its position on this recommendation and provide a response to this final report that meets the intent of the recommendation.

RECOMMENDATION 2

We recommend that the District of Columbia Housing Authority Director develop and implement an accounting system that can separately track costs for HOPE VI Program activities.

DCHA Response

DCHA management disagrees with the recommendation. They state that the current DCHA accounting system provides the necessary linkage of HOPE VI grant allocations and expenditures.

Figure 10–1 *continues*

OIG No. 01-2-25PH(c)
Final Report

FINDINGS AND RECOMMENDATIONS

OIG Comment

As shown in our report, seven distinct funds were deposited into one bank account. DCHA could not provide a reconciliation report to identify the sources of disbursements for HOPE VI activities. DCHA commingled HOPE VI grant funds with other types of funds into one bank account, and its system of recordkeeping could not separately account for HOPE VI Program expenditures. Once funds were deposited into DCHA's General Depository Operating Account, an adequate audit trail did not exist to enable the auditors to determine how the actual drawdowns were used. Using DCHA's accounting system, we tried to track and identify specific HOPE VI income and expenditures by project, but were unsuccessful. We concluded that DCHA's system of fund accounting could not be used to separately account for HOPE VI project funds and expenditures. We request that DCHA reconsider its position on this recommendation and provide a response to this final report that meets the intent of the recommendation.

Figure 10–1 *continued*

- Ignoring the goals and objectives as stated in the proposal
- Implementing a project in a manner other than the one described in the methodology section of the original proposal
- Violating any rules or regulations outlined in the terms and conditions of the grant
- Falsifying data collected as part of the project evaluation
- Inaccurate programmatic and/or fiscal reports
- Ignoring the submittal deadlines for programmatic and/or fiscal reports
- Neglecting to submit the programmatic, fiscal, or final reports as required by the funder

Possible Consequences of Mismanagement

Grantors have several options they can exercise when there is proof that a grantee has mismanaged a grant. These options range from withholding grant funds in the midst of the project implementation, requiring a grantee to repay funds that were mismanaged, and in the worst case, pursuing criminal charges and prosecuting a grantee. Most often, funders will require grantees to develop a corrective plan of action if mismanagement is uncovered and will monitor their progress following it.

In addition to the immediate consequences, grantees should remember that grantors often interact professionally. Even if the mismanagement is not publicized, it is possible that other grantors will find out about the occurrence. Mismanagement findings seriously damage the credibility of a grantee and may result in difficulties securing future funding from other funders. Some federal funders include a question on the grant application asking if the applicant owes any funds to the government, and if they do, applicants must describe the circumstances.

Case Studies of Mismanagement

The following case studies illustrate several types of mismanagement and show that both grantees and grantors at the state and federal level can fail to manage grants.

Case Study No. 1 Colorado Homeland Security Program

The audit of the state of Colorado Homeland Security Program (see **Figure 10–2**) is an example of mismanagement of grants on a state level. As the report describes, Colorado was doing a poor job of managing Department of Homeland Security grants. This is an interesting example of a *grantor* who was distributing grant awards to grantees throughout the state while mismanaging its own efforts as a recipient of federal funds.

DEPARTMENT OF HOMELAND SECURITY
Office of Inspector General

Audit of the State of Colorado Homeland Security Grant Program

OIG-08-16   **December 2007**

Figure 10–2 *Colorado Audit of Homeland Security report.*
Source: Office of Inspector General, U.S. Department of Homeland Security.

Colorado's Grant Management Efforts Need Improvement

Colorado needs to improve internal controls and management of its homeland security program to ensure the accuracy of recorded transactions and to certify sub-grantee compliance with federal and state requirements. Further, staff members managing the grant programs were few in number and not sufficiently trained, and thus sub-grantee monitoring efforts were ineffective.

The State of Colorado, as a grantee, is responsible for establishing and maintaining accounting systems, internal controls, and accounting records to properly account for grant activities. In addition, the state is responsible for managing the grant programs to ensure: 1) the success of grant applications review and award processes, 2) the eligibility and supportability of claims and cost reimbursements, and 3) sub-grantees' grant management practices conform to state and federal guidelines.

Ineffective Internal Controls

The state lacked effective internal controls for managing its homeland security grant program. Specifically:

- Federal drawdowns were not reviewed for accuracy and the state drew down cash in excess of needs. In two instances, the state initiated cash drawdowns of about $4 million in excess of needs but did not detect or correct the error until weeks after the transactions took place. In addition, the state earned about $11,555 in interest from excess drawdowns. State officials agreed to forward the interest to the federal government and to strengthen their procedures to ensure cash drawdowns are not in excess of needs.

Figure 10–2 *continues*

- Cash advances to sub-grantees were not monitored to ensure compliance with federal cash management requirements. The state was unaware that certain cash payments to sub-grantees were not for immediate needs. In one instance, a sub-grantee earned $5,460 in interest from a cash advance but did not forward the interest earned to the state or to the federal government. The 2005 State Auditor's report identified this weakness and recommended recovery of an unspecified amount of interest earned by sub-grantees during a 9-month period. However, the state did not take action on the recommendation because the related sub-grantee awards had been closed.

- Grants management reports generated from the state's "Oracle" database were not reviewed for accuracy and completeness. We identified errors in the reports that had not been detected or corrected. State officials agreed that the reports included errors and planned to update the programming and to monitor accuracy.

- Inventories of grant-funded equipment were incomplete or not maintained. The state's inventory database did not reflect all equipment purchased with homeland security and UASI grant funds, and the sub-grantees we visited either kept incomplete inventory records or kept no records at all. In addition, not all sub-grantees maintained adequate inventories of sensitive security equipment, such as portable radios and critical first responder equipment.

- Sub-grantees accounted for some management and administrative costs as direct program costs, and the state did not have procedures in place to ensure that reimbursements for management and administrative costs remained below or at the percentage allowable under the grants. Sub-grantees' accounting records showed that the administrative tasks of a grant coordinator and tasks associated with general computer equipment were recorded as direct program costs instead of management and administrative costs. In addition, sub-grantees did not specifically separate claimed management and administrative costs by grant effort or year. Thus, the state did not have an accurate record of management and administrative costs relative to a specific grant and a specific year.

In addition, management and administrative costs claimed by the state included a charge of 20 % of the salaries paid to seven state field managers. These managers assisted the state in providing field support in all areas of emergency management. The state did not monitor the employees' efforts or the benefits they provided to the homeland security grant program.

Figure 10–2 *continued*

- Established grant application, review, and award processes were not always understood or followed. For example, the state awarded $1.5 million to a state agency to acquire Colorado's Multi Agency Coordination Center – a project not eligible under the FY 2004 State Homeland Security Grant Program. The State Auditor and G&T questioned this transaction; and the state has since returned the funds to G&T. However, some state officials still believe the transaction was proper and that the state should have been allowed to retain the funds. We confirmed that in this instance the state did not follow grant award protocols and awarded the grant funds for an ineligible purpose. See Appendix E for a chronology of key events on this issue.

- The state did not ensure that funds were spent within the stated grant performance period. G&T's financial management guide provides that funds not properly obligated by the recipient within the grant performance period will lapse and revert to G&T. Instead of enforcing this requirement, the state routinely granted time extensions to sub-grantees or allowed transfers of costs from recently awarded grants to older grants to exhaust expiring funds.

- The state did not perform analytical reviews of grant applications to ensure the adequacy of planned grant expenditures and cost estimates. Grant estimates were generally overstated, resulting in surplus funds at the sub-grantee because actual costs were less than budgeted. Unlike state agencies that received homeland security funding from the state, most of the other sub-grantees kept the extra funds and used them for other projects. In some cases, they purchased items in numbers that exceeded those authorized in the grant agreement. In other instances, sub-grantees re-directed the funds by making transfers among budget line items; e.g., applying unused exercise and training funds to pay for equipment, supplies, and management and administrative costs.

Insufficient Number of Trained Staff

State employees managing homeland security and UASI grant programs were few in number and were not sufficiently trained. High employee turnover hampered the state's ability to manage these grant programs and monitor sub-grantee spending.

In September 2006 when this audit started, seven individuals accomplished homeland security grant management functions within the State Administrative Agency on a full- or part-time basis. Those employees included a recently hired State Administrative Agency Director, a Branch Chief, a Program Administrator, a trainee, a part-time grant technician, an

Figure 10–2 *continues*

accountant, and a temporary employee hired to conduct sub-grantee site visits and monitoring. As of November 2006, five of the seven employees remained. The State Administrative Agency Director and Program Administrator continued managing the grants, the accountant processed grant claims on a part time basis, and two employees, borrowed from other departments, processed incoming grant information. The borrowed employees had no formal grant management training, and one employee had no prior experience in grant operations.

As of May 2007, a new acting Division of Emergency Management Director (State Administrative Agency) and Branch Chief (filled by promoting the Program Administrator) remained as the only permanent employees involved in homeland security grants management. While the State Administrative Agency continued grant operations with one employee borrowed from another department, the lack of adequately trained staff impacted grant management operations and resulted in overall weak internal controls for managing program activities. In addition, officials from the all-hazards regions expressed dissatisfaction with the State Administrative Agency in that they had difficulty obtaining adequate and timely grant technical support.

Sub-grantee Monitoring Efforts Were Not Effective

The State Administrative Agency performed limited on-site, sub-grantee monitoring visits during FYs 2003 through 2005. Those visits were conducted on an add-hoc basis and reviews were limited to verifying the delivery and physical location of equipment purchased under the grants. The State Administrative Agency did not perform any on-site monitoring reviews of grant financial management practices until FY 2006. Despite its current efforts to expand the depth and breadth of on-site sub-grantee monitoring, deficiencies remain in the State Administrative Agency's monitoring process.

The State Administrative Agency developed a formal sub-grantee monitoring guide that included specific steps for evaluating grant financial management practices and for verifying equipment purchases during on site monitoring visits. Using its guide, the State Administrative Agency completed monitoring reviews of the 9 all-hazards regions, 16 state agencies, and the Denver urban area in FY 2006 but reported no adverse findings. However, State Administrative Agency records supporting its on site monitoring efforts and our reviews at selected sub-grantee locations disclosed deficiencies in the monitoring process.

- State records generally did not include documentation to support the adequacy and thoroughness of the monitoring. The completed monitoring guides included minor comments and checkmarks that

Figure 10–2 *continued*

indicated a step was completed, but no explanations were provided to describe the details of the work. The employee who completed the reviews explained that the purpose of the site visits was primarily to provide technical support. This individual further explained that discrepancies observed in grant management were resolved in the field; thus, they were not recorded or disclosed in the sub-grantees' site monitoring reports.

- Our review of financial management practices of some sub-grantees produced different results. As noted in this finding and other areas of this report, sub-grantees did not always comply with grant financial management practices. We identified deficiencies with cash management, procurement, equipment inventories, and general grant compliance.

Comments from state officials. State officials agreed that grant management efforts need improvement and explained that the state has taken steps to correct the internal control weaknesses discussed in this finding. With regard to management and administrative costs, they said additional controls have been introduced with the 2006 grant awards including steps to discontinue routinely charging 20% of the field managers' salaries to the grants. Instead, they plan to charge only the actual time spent by the managers on program activities. They also said that transferring costs from recently awarded grants to older grants was done on an exception basis. The state officials we talked to said that the state is planning to: (1) hire two employees to help manage homeland security and UASI grant programs, (2) develop a training checklist for new staff by June 1, 2007, (3) establish a training program for all staff by August 1, 2007, and (4) hire a financial compliance officer to improve state monitoring of sub-grantee activities.

Expenditures Not Always in Compliance With Grant Requirements

We reviewed the propriety of $26.9 million in homeland security and UASI grant expenditures and questioned about $7.8 million in costs claimed against those grants. The costs we questioned relate to the potential supplanting of state or local funds with federal funds ($3,900,000), commingling of grant program funding ($3,457,553), paying ineligible construction costs ($252,235), and paying other unallowable costs ($229,508). Appendix F summarizes the costs we questioned by grant program and grant year.

Office of Management and Budget Circular A-87, *Cost Principles for State, Local, and Indian Tribal Governments*, 2 CFR Part 225, requires that costs charged to the grants (federal awards) must be: a) allocable to federal awards

Figure 10–2 *continues*

and b) comply with any limitations set forth in the terms and conditions of the federal awards, such as grantor (i.e., G&T) guidelines and grant requirements.

Potential Supplanting of Grant Funds

G&T guidelines and grant regulations prohibit the use of federal funds to supplant state or local funds appropriated for objectives similar to grant purposes. Specifically, the Department of Justice (DOJ), Office of Justice Programs financial guide, part II, chapter 3 – standards for financial systems/supplanting, specifies that federal funds must not replace those (state/local) funds that have been appropriated for the same purpose... and the applicant or grantee will be required to supply documentation demonstrating that the reduction in non-Federal resources occurred for reasons other than the receipt or expected receipt of federal funds[3]. Also, Title 28, Code of Federal Regulation, Part 66, *Uniform Administrative Requirements for Grants and Cooperative Agreements to State and Local Governments*, Section 66.40, requires grantees to monitor grant and sub-grant supported activities to assure compliance with applicable federal requirements and to ensure that performance goals are achieved.

The North Central Region expended $3.9 million of FY 2004 Homeland Security Grant Program funds for infrastructure equipment associated with a digital trunked radio system (system). Section 24-30-908.5 of the Colorado revised statutes establishes the state's Public Safety Communications Trust Fund to pay for the acquisition and maintenance for public safety communications equipment, including the digital trunked radio system components. Using trust funds, the state purchased two of the three radio system controllers needed for its communications infrastructure and the region purchased the third controller. Region officials stated that the state's communications infrastructure required the third controller for system expansion and would allow: 1) for additional repeater sites to be added to the statewide system, 2) communications centers to directly access the system without backroom equipment, and 3) agencies utilizing non-compatible equipment to create easy points of access between communications centers.

Records supporting the purchase of the third controller and discussions with state officials indicated that the region and the state agreed that title to the controller would transfer from the region to the state after acquisition and the equipment would become part of Colorado's overall communications infrastructure. However, the region did not transfer the equipment to the state but transferred title to a local non-profit organization. This non-profit organization is a consortium of government agencies that manage

---

[3] DOJ, Office of Justice Programs, provided financial management support and monitoring of homeland security grants through fiscal year 2005.

Figure 10–2 *continued*

communications issues for the State of Colorado and is organized exclusively for the purpose of managing, promoting, and propagating the Colorado Statewide Digital Trunked Radio System. There was no indication in the files that the region sought or received approval from the state or G&T. Regarding the transfer, the region's Board of Directors minutes stated, "...all operating and maintenance expenses will be the responsibility of the local non-profit and if the local non-profit is unable to fulfill ownership requirements in the future, the zone controller will be turned over to the State." Further, the region's procurement did not conform to federal, state, and local acquisition requirements inasmuch as the acquisition was sole source procurement and was not reviewed or approved by responsible officials.

With regard to applying federal funds to purchase the third controller, a state official explained that homeland security grants allowed for the expenditure and therefore using the trust fund monies was not necessary. We did not verify the balance of the trust fund and related budgets as of the date the controller was acquired because the Colorado State Auditor was in the process of auditing the trust fund. We recommend that G&T contact the Colorado State Auditor and determine the nature of the transaction. We also recommend that, if state funds were supplanted with federal funds, G&T de-obligate the $3.9 million of 2004 grant funds applied to the purchase of the third controller.

Commingling of Grant Funds

Federal regulations require sub-grantees to obtain approval prior to transferring grant funds among direct cost categories or among separately budgeted programs, functions, or activities, when such transfers would exceed 10% of the total approved budget whenever the grantor's share exceeds $100,000. These regulations also require sub-grantees to obtain prior approval for revisions to project scope or objectives and provide two other instances when sub-grantees must obtain prior approval for fund or budget transfers. In addition, G&T's financial guide requires separate accounting for each grant award and prohibits commingling funds on either program-by-program or project-by-project bases. The guide also specifies that funds specifically budgeted and/or received for one project may not be used to support another.

We question $3.4 million in transfers among grants because prior written approval had not been obtained from G&T. Of the amount questioned, we identified $2 million at the Denver UASI and $1.4 million attributable to other sub-grantees. The transfers were initiated because: 1) older grants had reached the end of the grant performance period and unspent funds were due to expire; and 2) the sub-grantees did not want to return the unspent funds to

Figure 10–2 *continues*

the state. These transfers undermine the appropriateness of the grant award process and do not ensure: 1) appropriate expenditure of grant funds; 2) effective management of G&T grant resources; and 3) programmatic and fiscal accountability. In addition, we question how the sub-grantees plan to use the grant funds awarded under current grant programs since approved project expenditures under the current awards were defrayed by funds transferred from the expiring awards.

Ineligible Construction Costs

The Denver UASI used $252,235 of grant funds to pay for ineligible construction costs. Specifically, the Denver UASI used $116,427 of the FY 2003 grant to construct a foundation, stairs, and a room for interoperable equipment at one site and $135,808 of the FY 2004 grant to construct a telecommunications room at the City of Denver's new fire station. G&T program guidelines specifically prohibit the use of grant funds for construction or renovation of facilities.

Unallowable Costs

The Denver UASI claimed $236,606 in consulting fees that were not prorated among benefiting activities. The fees related to a City of Denver interoperable communications project that was funded with UASI and DOJ grants and with City of Denver funds. Denver UASI and City of Denver records show that $236,606 in fees was charged to the FY 2004 UASI grant although the grant only represented 3% of the overall project objective and costs. As such, only $7,098 of the fees was attributable to the UASI grant ($236,606 x 3%) and the other $229,508 is questioned as an unallowable cost ($236,606 x 97%). Office of Management and Budget Circular A-87, G&T's financial guidelines, and the Office for Justice Programs financial guide require sub-grantees to maintain adequate documentation of grant expenditures and allocate the cost of goods or services to cost objectives in accordance with relative benefits received.

Comments from state officials. The state officials who reviewed this finding did not agree that the cost of the digital trunked radio controller should be questioned and explained that the state infrastructure did not require the equipment. Therefore, they concluded that using homeland security grant funds to purchase the controller was not supplanting local funds. They agreed that the equipment was transferred to the non-profit without state or G&T approval, but did not provide a comment about procurement standards that the sub-grantee failed to follow. The state also noted that it plans to resolve remaining issues as follows: 1) UASI transfer of $317,451 among grants will be resolved by December 31, 2007, 2) ineligible construction costs of

Figure 10–2 *continued*

$252,235 will be resolved by October 31, 2007, and 3) unallowable costs of $236,606 will be resolved by October 31, 2007. The state acknowledged that transfers between newer grants and older grants have occurred but only on an exception basis. Since we completed the review of costs after our fieldwork, state officials did not have an opportunity to comment on the $3.1 million in transfers among grants that were initiated by state grant administrators.

Funding Was Not Always Allocated To High Risk Projects

From FY 2003 to FY 2006, Colorado improved its methodology to ensure that grant funds were allocated to the state's highest priorities; and in FY 2007, the state continued to make improvements. However, the state did not always reallocate surplus or excess grant funding to projects with the highest priorities. Colorado's State Homeland Security Strategy and federal homeland security program guidelines identify risk as the primary factor to consider when allocating grant funds. The state should use planning and data from multiple sources to identify and fund the highest priority activities on a statewide basis. This ensures that the state's homeland security preparedness contributes to national preparedness goals.

Documentation for the FY 2005 homeland security grant program showed that the state reallocated about $600,000 reverted from a canceled state project to eight of the nine all-hazards regions but documentation did not support that the funds went to projects with a high statewide priority. Further, the state did not monitor sub-grantees to ensure that they returned excess funds resulting from over estimated costs in grant budgets. While state guidelines require prior approval for reusing excess funds, local sub-grantees did not comply with the requirement, and the state did not enforce it. For example, two of the five all-hazards regions visited used over $250,000 in excess funds to acquire radio equipment in excess of the number approved in their grant budgets. The state only became aware of the transactions when the regions submitted the costs for reimbursement. Finally, the state either approved or allowed sub-grantees to reallocate grant funds within budget line items without considering high-priority needs on a statewide basis.

<u>Comments from state officials</u>. State officials agreed with this finding and noted that equipment prices fluctuated due to market conditions. These officials noted that previously, the regions operated autonomously and could use unexpended funds to pay for the next highest regional priority once approved by the regional board of directors. However, because of the Governor's interest in implementing a clearer homeland security strategy, the State Administrative Agency is strengthening methods for identifying and funding the regions' highest priority projects.

Figure 10–2 *continued*

Case Study No. 2 Reading First Program

In the Reading First Program, the OIG final inspection report (see **Figure 10–3**) indicates that the grantor, the U.S. Department of Education, mishandled several aspects of the grantee selection process, which, in turn, affected the use of federal funds. As the table of contents shows, there are findings related to the review panel of the grant. These include questions about the selection of panel members and the screening for possible conflicts of interest. The findings also discuss the favoritism towards vendors of reading programs who stood to gain profits from being included in budgets of proposals that were funded. Proposals for projects using reading vendors who were not favored by the U.S. Department of Education staff were often unfunded.

Case Study No. 3 Manvel, TX Police Department

The U.S. Department of Justice Audit Report of the Manvel, Texas, Police Department is filled with findings related to the mismanagement of the Funding Accelerated for Smaller Towns grant program and funding received from the Universal Hiring Program. The executive summary (see **Figure 10–4**) shows that several examples of mismanagement in the grant programs included commingling of funds, violating the terms and conditions of the Funding Accelerated for Smaller Towns grant regarding community policing, no submittal or late submittal of reports, a lack of accounting for grant revenue and expenditures, and inflating budget numbers in the original proposal.

Case Study No. 4 School District of Lancaster

In 2004, the Pennsylvania Department of the Auditor General released a 70-page report that revealed wasteful spending and poor tax administrative oversight in the School District of Lancaster. According to the report's table of contents and introduction and background (see **Figure 10–5**), the district had mismanaged federal funds, the selection process for consultants, and the use of credit cards and cellular phones. The auditor general concluded that from 1997 to 2003, nearly 70% of the $3.2 million spent on educational consultants was for services that were not included in a written contract. Additionally, the consultants were hand selected by staff without school board or business office staff input into the selection process.

During the time period investigated, the district was run by two superintendents. In 2003, the second superintendent hired his sister, girlfriend, brother-in-law, and close friend to provide consulting and grant administration services to the district. The Auditor General's Office also found that the district failed to manage a program that was supported by federal funds. The superintendent was charged with mail fraud by the U.S. Attorney's Office as a result of an investigation conducted by the Federal Bureau of Investigation. He pled guilty to the charges in September 2004 and was given a 2-year prison sentence.

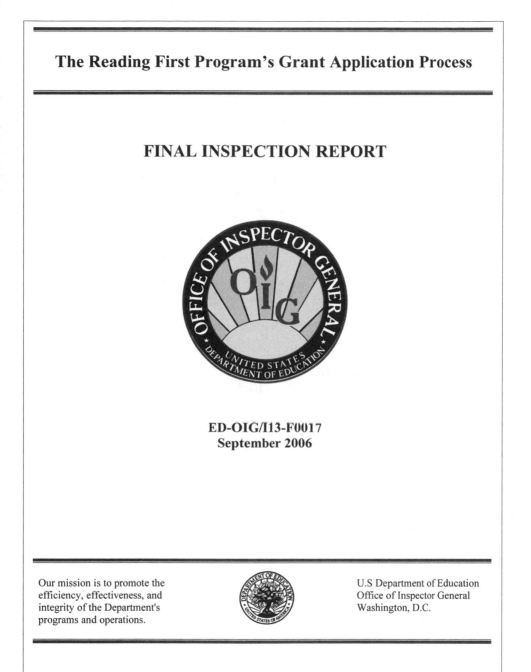

The Reading First Program's Grant Application Process

FINAL INSPECTION REPORT

ED-OIG/I13-F0017
September 2006

Our mission is to promote the
efficiency, effectiveness, and
integrity of the Department's
programs and operations.

U.S Department of Education
Office of Inspector General
Washington, D.C.

(continues)

Figure 10–3 *Office of Inspector General Reading First Program report.*
Source: *Office of Inspector General, U.S. Department of Education.*

Statements that managerial practices need improvements, as well as other conclusions and recommendations in this report represent the opinions of the Office of Inspector General. Determinations of corrective action to be taken will be made by the appropriate Department of Education officials.

In accordance with the Freedom of Information Act (5 U.S.C. § 552), reports issued by the Office of Inspector General are available, if requested, to members of the press and general public to the extent information contained therein is not subject to exemptions in the Act.

Figure 10–3 *continued*

TABLE OF CONTENTS

Figure 10–3 *continues*

Final Report
ED-OIG/I13-F0017

EXECUTIVE SUMMARY

The objectives of our inspection were to:

1. Determine if the Department of Education (Department, ED, or USDE) selected the expert review panel in accordance with the No Child Left Behind Act of 2001 (NCLB), Section 1203(c) and if the Department adequately screened the panel members for possible conflict of interest issues;

2. Determine if the expert review panel adequately documented its reasons for stating that an application was unready for funding; and

3. Determine if the expert review panel reviewed the applications in accordance with established criteria and applied the criteria consistently.

The selection of the expert review panel was not in compliance with the law because the Department failed to ensure that each State application was reviewed by a properly constituted panel.

Although not required, the Department developed a process to screen expert review panelists for conflicts of interest; however, the Department's process was not effective. We identified six panelists whose resumes revealed significant professional connections to a teaching methodology that requires the use of a specific reading program. The Department did not identify any of these connections in its conflict of interest screening process; therefore, it would not have been in a position to deal with the potential conflict raised by these connections should a State have included this program in its application.

The expert review panel adequately documented its reasons for stating that an application was unready for funding; however, the Department substituted a Department-created report for the panel's comments. As a result, the Department did not follow its own guidance for the peer review process. Therefore, States did not have the benefit of the expert review panel's comments and were not always able to quickly or effectively address problems in their applications. Additionally, we found that five of the State applications we reviewed were funded without documentation that they met all of the criteria for approval. The Department has not provided any documentation that would indicate the subpanels approved the final applications for these States.

The expert review panel appears to have reviewed the applications in accordance with criteria developed by the Department and applied the criteria consistently; however, the criteria developed by the Department included language that was not based on the statutory language. As a result, State applications were forced to meet standards that were not required by the statute.

Figure 10–3 *continued*

Final Report
ED-OIG/I13-F0017

In the course of answering our three objectives, we found that Department officials obscured the statutory requirements of the Elementary and Secondary Education Act of 1965 (ESEA), as amended by NCLB; acted in contravention of the Government Accountability Office's (GAO) *Standards for Internal Control in the Federal Government*; and took actions that call into question whether they violated the prohibitions included in the Department of Education Organization Act (DEOA). The DEOA at §3403(b) prohibits Department officials from exercising any direction, supervision, or control over the curriculum or program of instruction of any educational institution, school, or school system.

Specifically, we found that the Department:

- Developed an application package that obscured the requirements of the statute;
- Took action with respect to the expert review panel process that was contrary to the balanced panel composition envisioned by Congress;
- Intervened to release an assessment review document without the permission of the entity that contracted for its development;
- Intervened to influence a State's selection of reading programs; and
- Intervened to influence reading programs being used by local educational agencies (LEAs) after the application process was completed.

These actions demonstrate that the program officials failed to maintain a control environment that exemplifies management integrity and accountability.

We recommend that the Assistant Secretary for the Office of Elementary and Secondary Education (OESE):

1) Develop internal management policies and procedures for OESE program offices that address when legal advice will be solicited from the Office of the General Counsel (OGC) and how discussions between OGC and the program staff will be resolved to ensure that programs are managed in compliance with applicable laws and regulations.
2) In consultation with OGC, evaluate OESE's processes for assessing potential conflict of interest questions, when a panel review process is used, and make those improvements necessary to strengthen the processes.
3) Review all Reading First applications to determine whether all criteria for funding have been met.
4) Review the management and staff structure of the Reading First program office and make changes, as appropriate, to ensure that the program is managed and implemented consistent with the statutory requirements of NCLB.
5) Request that OGC develop guidance for OESE on the prohibitions imposed by §3403(b) of the Department of Education Organization Act.
6) When similar new initiatives are approved by Congress, rely upon an internal advisory committee, which includes representatives from other OESE programs, OGC, and the Department's Risk Management Team, to provide feedback on program implementation issues and ensure coordination in the delivery of similar or complimentary Department programs.

Figure 10–3 *continues*

Final Report
ED-OIG/I13-F0017

7) Rely upon the internal advisory committee to:
   a. Determine whether the implementation of Reading First harmed the Federal interest and what course of action is required to resolve any issues identified; and
   b. Ensure that future programs, including other programs for which the Department is considering using Reading First as a model, have internal controls in place to prevent similar problems from occurring.
8) Convene a discussion with a broad range of state and local education representatives to discuss issues with Reading First as part of the reauthorization process.

Figure 10–3 *continued*

U.S. DEPARTMENT OF JUSTICE

Audit Report

Office of Community Oriented Policing Services

Manvel Police Department

Manvel, Texas

GR-80-99-003

December 21, 1998

* * * * *

EXECUTIVE SUMMARY

The Office of the Inspector General, Audit Division, has completed an audit of two grants awarded by the U.S. Department of Justice, Office of Community Oriented Policing Services, to the City of Manvel Police Department, Manvel, Texas. The City received a grant of $73,361 to hire one officer under the Funding Accelerated for Smaller Towns (FAST) program, a supplemental award of $183,947 to hire three officers under the Universal Hiring Program (UHP), and a second identical UHP supplemental award of $183,947 to hire three additional officers, for a total of seven officers. As of September 30, 1998, the City of Manvel (City) had not accepted the second UHP supplemental award. The purpose of the additional grant officers was to enhance community policing.

(continues)

Figure 10–4 *U.S. Department of Justice Audit Report of the Manvel, Texas, Police Department.*
Source: *U.S. Department of Justice.*

The City did not comply with the terms and conditions of the grants. Specifically, the City failed to implement, enhance, or augment community policing efforts with the awarded grant funds or develop a formal retention plan for retaining the grant-funded positions. Therefore, we are questioning $73,361 of the FAST grant and $72,063 of the UHP supplemental funds.

We found the following discrepancies with regard to meeting grant conditions:

- City officials overstated entry-level salary and fringe benefits in the FAST grant application by $19,209, even though they had been told that these costs were inflated.
- The City requested reimbursements and advances based on inflated budgeted salary and fringe benefits rather than actual costs, thereby depleting the FAST funds in 27 months.
- The City drew excess grant funds of $17,917 on the UHP award and placed the funds in the City's general fund.
- The City did not implement, enhance, or augment community policing.
- The City did not have procedures to ensure that accurate, actual grant revenues and expenditures were properly accounted for.
- The City commingled FAST grant funds with other Federal funds.
- The City drew $54,146 for UHP grant-funded officers from January 1, 1997, through September 30, 1997, even though officers were not sworn in until September 30, 1997.
- The grant-funded officers were not trained in community policing.
- The City did not annually decrease the Federal share rate in requests for reimbursements or advances.
- The City did not develop any type of retention plan for continuing the employment of the grant-funded officers at the end of the grant period.
- The Police Department's Annual Report for 1996 was submitted late and described community policing activities that could not be verified.
- The Police Department submitted an Officer Progress Report for 1996 that described community policing activities that could not be substantiated.
- The City submitted Financial Status Reports that were not supported by the City's accounting records.
- The City did not submit Financial Status Reports for the second quarter of 1998.
- The Police Department did not submit four Officer Progress Reports for 1997.
- The Police Department did not submit an Annual Report for 1997.

These items are discussed in the Findings and Recommendations section of the report. Our scope and methodology appear in Appendix I, and our schedule of dollar-related findings is at Appendix II.

Figure 10–4 *continued*

COMMONWEALTH OF PENNSYLVANIA
Department of the Auditor General

SUMMARY REPORT:

THE SCHOOL DISTRICT OF THE CITY OF LANCASTER

December 2004

(continues)

Figure 10–5 *Pennsylvania Department of the Auditor General report of the School District of Lancaster.*
Source: *Pennsylvania Department of the Auditor General.*

TABLE OF CONTENTS

Figure 10–5 *continued*

Tables

Figure 10–5 *continues*

INTRODUCTION AND BACKGROUND

The Department of the Auditor General (the Department) conducts audits of school districts pursuant to its authority and responsibility under The Fiscal Code.[1] In December 2003, the Department's Office of Special Investigations (OSI) received complaints of alleged misuse of funds and conflicts of interest relating to the hiring of consultants by the then-superintendent of the School District of Lancaster (the school district). OSI then began an investigation.

In January 2004, media reports began to appear concerning the allegations against the school district superintendent. During the same month, the Department learned that the Federal Bureau of Investigation (FBI) was investigating the allegations against the superintendent and the school district announced that an internal investigation of the use of consultants was being conducted by an independent accounting firm. The superintendent resigned on January 27, 2004.

In September 2004, a Criminal Information charging former superintendent Ricardo Curry with mail fraud was filed in the United States District Court for the Eastern District of Pennsylvania by the United States Attorney's Office.[2] On September 28, 2004, Curry pleaded guilty to charges in the Criminal Information. Curry is scheduled to be sentenced on January 14, 2005.

The OSI investigation focused on (1) consulting services; (2) the Cultural Translator Program; (3) credit cards; and (4) use of cellular telephones. Our investigation was conducted in cooperation with the federal inquiry. During our investigation, the Department received other complaints and discovered other questionable matters concerning school district activities. Those complaints for which an investigation was warranted will be addressed in a future OSI report. The others are being referred to the school district or to the appropriate agency, for action and/or further review. One matter, relating to records of financial interests reports required to be filed by school district officials, is addressed in this report.

OSI's investigation included interviews of current and former school district officials and employees, interviews of consultants and vendors and reviews of school district records and records of vendors. The period of our review generally covered the 1997-1998 school year through the 2003-2004 school year unless otherwise noted. Due to the federal investigation, some records and individuals were unavailable to us or did not become available until late in the investigation.

---

[1] 72 P.S. § 403.
[2] United States of America v. Ricardo Curry, Criminal No. 04-560.

Figure 10–5 *continued*

During the period covered by the inquiry, the school district had several changes of management-level officials, including superintendents and business managers. Where necessary for clarity, former superintendents are identified by name. Former Superintendent Phillips, who served from 1998 to January 2003, was interviewed.[3] Former Superintendent Curry, who served from April 2003 to January 2004, declined to be interviewed when we made an initial attempt to do so in January 2004. He has not been available to be interviewed since that time.

On November 19, 2004, the draft summary report was made available to school district officials to provide the school district with the opportunity to submit a response. The school district's complete response was received on November 25, 2004, and is included in the report on pp. 57-62. Portions of the response that relate to individual findings are also presented in the sections of the report concerning the finding, together with the Department's comments. The school district's implementation of its corrective actions will be monitored by the Department in future regular audits.

A copy of the draft report was also provided to former Superintendent Phillips. She sent a response, which has also been included in the report at pp. 63-64, together with the Department's comments related to the response.

---

[3] Former Superintendent Phillips served as Secretary of the Pennsylvania Department of Education from January 2003 until July 2004.

Figure 10–5 *continues*

EXECUTIVE SUMMARY

The school district failed to manage the selection, monitoring and oversight of educational consultants.

The school district failed to manage a Cultural Translator Program costing approximately $382,000 obtained from federal grant funds.

The school district failed to manage the use of credit cards.

The school district failed to manage the use of cellular telephones.

The school district did not have in its records Statements of Financial Interests required to be filed by school district officials in accordance with the Ethics Act.

RECOMMENDATIONS

1. The school district should immediately develop and implement policies and procedures relating to educational consultants; implementation should be closely monitored by the school board; monitoring should include the full participation of the business manager and regular oversight by the school district's independent auditor. (Finding No. 1.)

2. The school district should require all educational consultants providing services to the school district to have a written agreement or contract. (Finding No. 1.)

3. Terms and conditions of consultant agreements should include:

   - A listing of other payments to which consultants are entitled, including travel expenses and reimbursement for supplies.

   - The time period of agreements, including start and ending dates.

   - A description of information to be presented on invoices, such as details of specific services, dates and places of service, and references to required documentation, such as reports.

   - The consultant's name, address, telephone number, e-mail address and federal identification number or Social Security number.

Figure 10–5 *continued*

- A statement of required licensing and professional certifications and authorizations/waivers relating to criminal record background checks.

- A statement that agreements are contingent upon approval by the school board.

- A statement that the consultant is subject to periodic review or audit of services by school district personnel, state auditors, and/or independent auditors and that consultants must provide all requested records and documentation to auditors in a timely manner as a condition of the agreement.

(Finding No. 1.)

4. The school district should review all consultants currently providing services to the school district to ensure that the services are being provided, charges are reasonable and contract requirements are met. (Finding No. 1.)

5. Written agreements should be obtained for all current consultants. (Finding No. 1.)

6. The school district should appoint a full-time qualified administrator to monitor consultant services. The administrator should report to the business manager or the appropriate committee of the school board and should provide periodic reports to the school board concerning consultants and their services. (Finding No. 1.)

7. Consultants' invoices should be reviewed and approved for payment by the Business office. (Finding No. 1.)

8. The administrator should sign off on consultants' invoices prior to their approval. (Finding No. 1)

9. No one with a personal or financial relationship to a school district official should be hired as a consultant without full disclosure of the nature of the relationship to the school board in writing and abstention of the school district official from any role in the hiring process. (Finding No. 1.)

10. The school district should conduct a detailed review of the 20 additional consultants for which former Superintendent Curry was the school district official who signed off on invoices or who dealt with the individual consultant. (Finding No. 1.)

11. The school district should obtain from the Shalom Partnership and other parties, including former superintendent Curry and law enforcement agencies, all records and other information concerning billings and charges for Cultural Translators, including timesheets, pay records, and names, addresses and background materials for all

Figure 10–5 *continues*

Cultural Translators, determine whether there is a reasonable basis for the charges, and seek reimbursement of all improper or undocumented charges. (Finding No. 2.)

12. The school district should adopt and enforce a policy that all persons performing services for the school district who may come into contact with students, including employees of a contractor, vendor and non-profit agencies, volunteers, consultants and temporary employees, obtain an up-to-date criminal record background check from the Pennsylvania State Police and all other background checks required by law. (Finding No. 2.)

13. The school district should review the appropriateness of the former Shalom Partnership grant administrator's continued involvement in school district activities in any capacity, including that of a contract employee. (Finding No. 2.)

14. The school district should establish, implement and enforce uniform district-wide policies and procedures regarding authorized credit card purchases. (Finding No. 3.)

15. The school district should ensure awareness and understanding of its credit card policies and procedures through the distribution of written materials and periodic training sessions for appropriate individuals, including authorized users, the business office staff, building principals and senior management officials. (Finding No. 3.)

16. The school district should differentiate between credit cards intended for use for purchases of supplies (generally referred to as "Purchasing Cards") and credit cards used for payment of travel expenses by individuals. The former should be assigned only to a specific and limited number of individuals with duties related to purchasing; the latter should be assigned only to officials and other employees who travel regularly, and who are responsible for making the payments for credit card charges themselves and then submitting claims for reimbursement to the school district for charges that are necessary and related to official school district business. (Finding No. 3.)

17. The school district should require all cardholders to reimburse the school district for all inappropriate purchases. (Finding No. 3.)

18. The school district should limit the number of credit cards and credit card users to the minimum necessary to conduct essential business and limit the vendors from which items can be purchased to those furnishing school supplies and other allowed items. (Finding No. 3.)

19. The school district should require approval by the school district technology office before purchasing technology-related items such as Palm Pilots, cellular telephones,

Figure 10–5 *continued*

computers and printers and maintain an inventory of such items to prevent loss or misuse. (Finding No. 3.)

20. The school district should prohibit purchases of meals and food by purchasing card holders and prohibit purchasing cards from being used for travel or other travel-related costs. (Finding No. 3.)

21. The school district should impose strict timeframes for reconciliation of monthly credit card statements. (Finding No. 3.)

22. The school district should require submission and retention of documentation to justify credit card purchases and require regular reports to the school board by the business office concerning credit card use, the number and identity of cardholders, letters, notices and other actions taken in regard to questioned and inappropriate credit card purchases, and reimbursement payments for inappropriate charges. (Finding No. 3.)

23. The school district should obtain an explanation of the justification for the questionable credit card charges, or obtain full and immediate repayment (or, where possible, the items purchased) from former Superintendent Curry, the former Director of Communications and the former McCaskey High School principal in connection with all improper credit card charges. (Finding No. 3.)

24. The school district should adopt and enforce policies and procedures for cellular telephones that include: evaluation of the justification for each cellular telephone assigned based on the user's duties; a specific limitation of use to official business; a requirement that monthly bills should be sent to users for review and written acknowledgement that calls were for official purposes and not for personal use; and a requirement that charges for calls identified as personal should be repaid to the school district within 30 days. (Finding No. 4.)

25. If no charge is listed for a cellular telephone call because it is included in the cellular telephone plan, the school district should establish a reasonable amount that users should be required to pay the school district for personal calls. (Finding No. 4.)

26. The school district should ensure that substantial misuse of a cellular telephone or failure to pay for personal calls should result in return of the equipment to the school district and appropriate disciplinary action. (Finding No. 4.)

27. The school board should ensure that all records of financial interests required to be kept in the school district in accordance with the Ethics Act are present and kept in a secure location; that they are reviewed regularly by the solicitor to ensure that all information required to be on file is present; and that the school district follow the

Figure 10–5 *continues*

direction and advice of the State Ethics Commission in regard to obtaining resubmission of missing SFIs. (Finding No. 5.)

Figure 10–5 *continued*

Chapter Summary

Managing grants can be a difficult task and can potentially lead to occurrences of unethical behavior. Knowing in advance what constitutes unethical behavior may cut down on this type of occurrence.

Grantees and grantors should strive to build a relationship on integrity and maintain an honest relationship with each other. Grantees must know that unethical behavior can have a variety of consequences, with the most serious being criminal prosecution.

Chapter 11

Problem Solving

What should a grantee do if he is experiencing any problems with grants management tasks? The only real answer is to contact the funder, discuss the situation, have some possible solutions prepared, and be open to suggestions from the funder. Grantees will create a risky situation if they make decisions on their own without prior consultation with the funder. For the most part, funders are willing to provide assistance to solve problems as they, too, want projects to succeed.

In addition to contacting the funder, grantees can also brainstorm with current and prior grantees to see if they had a similar problem when implementing a project. However, grantees should not rely solely on information from other grantees to decide how to solve their situation.

Other grantees who have received grants from a variety of funding sources can also be a good resource for coming up with possible solutions to the problems. Chances are they have also experienced a variety of issues with projects over the years and can be a source of helpful information. Grantees may want to contact individuals who are members of organizations such as the Association for Fundraising Professionals and the American Association of Grant Professionals for information and assistance.

Understanding unethical behavior in regard to managing grants is critical. As the information in Chapter 10 shows, grants mismanagement does not only apply to the misuse of grant funds. Web-based training offered by federal agencies or workshops by the National Grants Management Association may provide additional guidance for problematic situations.

Effective grants management is a critical piece of the grantsmanship process and should be practiced by every grantee, regardless of the amount of the grant award. Receiving grants creates an important relationship between the grantor and the grantee. Such a relationship can be vital to the mission and growth of organizations and provide valuable services to individuals around the world.